Together Apart

Two lives mirror German
history of the last seventy years

Renate Dietrich

This book is dedicated to my wonderful friend and cousin Ute, but a big thanks goes to Eileen as well, who made me write down our story.

Contents

1. Together again	1
2. Where we come from	3
3. With us were born two German states	8
4. "Nobody is thinking of building a wall."	15
5. From pen-pals to best of friends	19
6. Crossing-over	24
7. Going out shopping	28
8. Tell me what program you watch!	36
9. Girls will be girls	39
10. Getting into trouble	45
11. Weimar, Eisenach and Buchenwald – the different faces of Germany's history	48
12. The Swinging Sixties	58
13. Friends and more	63
14. Prague, August 1968	69
15. Are we grown-ups now or what?	83
16. The sixties and their politics	98
17. A Day in School	108
18. How not to become a spy	112

19. While we were separated	120
20. The Big Thaw	133
21. Picking up the thread	145
22. Re-discovering the town	152
23. The General Line	160
24. Food for Thought	167
25. What remains	172
26. What happened afterwards	189

1. **Together again**

So here I am again, looking up to the front door. The house looks well-kept as does the garden, which was already mature, when we played in it as children. More than thirteen years have passed since this door closed behind me for the last time. Then we had no idea that it would be a goodbye for such a long time.

When Michael and I came down the road leading into the town centre I recognized the corner, where we had to turn left, immediately. It was as though an in-built compass was guiding me to the right address.

When I had tried to call for the first time and the telephone was answered eventually the answering voice sounded so familiar, that I thought it was Ute. It came as a bit of a shock that this was her grown-up daughter, who was only a toddler when I saw them the last time.

How will it be when the door eventually opens? Will we feel awkward? Will we be disappointed because the long years have changed us so much that we have nothing in common any longer?

Anxiously I open the gate and ring the doorbell. They must have been waiting for us, the door opens so quickly. Ute and I fall into each other's arms. There is a lot of laughter. No tears. We can't stop telling each other how absolutely delighted we are. And that it is unbelievable. We are not the only ones who feel that way. "Unbelievable" is one of the most used expression in those months.

Eberhard grins and gives me a hug. He was already part of the family when we were separated. Michael on the other hand is a new factor. Of course, they know of him. I have mentioned him in my letter and on the telephone. Still there is the question how he would fit in. After all he is what in Germany still ranks very highly on the ladder of approval: a professor of physics!

I introduce him. The men shake hands formally. But I can sense that he appears much less frightening that they thought he would be.

We slowly make it to the living room. There is so much to tell. All these years! So much has happened. But very soon it feels as if Ute and I were never separated. We just fall back into a relationship which started when we were children, continued into our adulthood, was forcibly interrupted by history and now that the winds of change have blown us together again, can be continued as if we had spoken only yesterday. That it worked out like that is one of the wonders of my life.

2. Where we come from

Ute and I are nothing wonderful or even exceptional. However lately I realised that between us we cover a lot of German history of the last century. So, it might be worthwhile telling our story.

Our mothers were cousins, as their fathers, our grandfathers, were brothers. While I liked Ute's grandfather Hermann very much I was more in awe of mine, Karl Walther. My grandfather was a large man with a moustache which, while he was young, optimistically pointed upwards in an imitation of Kaiser Wilhelm's. After the First World War and with the Kaiser in exile that feeling of optimism must have vanished, because from then on, and while I knew him, his moustache always hung down and made him look a bit like a walrus. Hermann unlike his older brother was a short man with a lot of wrinkles in his face which came from smiling. In my memories he knew a lot and was always ready to tell a joke or a funny story.

They came from Kölleda, a small village in Thuringia, where their forefathers had been peasants. Both of us, Ute and I, own identical drawings of the house in which they grew up, very naive but moving sketches. A few years ago, Ute went in search of the house, but she could not find it. It might have been replaced by another building or renovated to the point of being simply unrecognisable.

Both brothers left their village. Hermann stayed in Thuringia and moved to Erfurt, the main city in the area. Karl ended up in Breslau in Silesia, where he got married and where my mother and her two brothers were born.

Karl and Hermann did fairly well in life despite their humble beginnings. Both built houses for their families (which was no small achievement, as at that time the overwhelming majority of the population in Germany could only afford rented accommodation). My mother's eldest brother, Karl jun., joined the armed forces and became an officer. My mother Erika and her younger brother Wolfgang both went to university.

Being born shortly after the First World War, our mothers and fathers grew up in the thirties and forties, when Germany was a fascist and racist dictatorship under Hitler and the NSDAP (Nationalsozialistische Deutsche Arbeiterpartei /National Socialistic German Worker's Party). When Hitler came to power Erika was 13 years old and Ute's mother Gerti was of about the same age.

I do not think that any of my mother's family were convinced Nazis but neither did they actively oppose. There was still a strong tradition in Germany and in this family to obey orders, to trust in and to conform to the authorities. Nevertheless, the family stood by Erika, when she decided that my father Ernst was the love of her life and that she was going to marry him.

Ernst came from a Jewish family and lived a precarious semi-disguised existence in Nazi Germany. Her family knew about his background, they knew that if he was ever found out, it could be dangerous for all of them, but nobody betrayed the young couple.

My parents got married in October 1944, coinciding with the horrible peak of terror against the Jews of Europe. After only two weeks of a strange kind of honeymoon under the fire of the approaching Russian front the young couple was separated. Only in 1948 did my father come back from Russian Prisoner of War camps. In contrast to many war-time marriages, which did not last, for my parents only death could part them. In 1999, when my mother died, my parents had been married for more than 54 years.

During the winter of 1944/45 it became more than obvious that the war would be lost. Nevertheless, all men between sixteen and sixty-five were now drawn into the army in a last desperate attempt to stem the tide. So, our grandfathers, who were in or approaching their sixties, had to become soldiers once more. With the men away at the Russian front and the fighting coming closer and closer Erika and her mother decided to flee from Silesia. The family had discussed their possibilities and had agreed on Hermann's house in Erfurt as a meeting point if they lost each other in the chaos of the eventual collapse. Fortunately, this house was not destroyed, so this was where my mother and my grandmother headed to seek temporary shelter and to wait for news from their men all of whom eventually were captured and imprisoned in Prisoner of War camps.

Thus, it happened that Erika and Gerti, the cousins, who had known each other from family visits and occasional joint holidays, lived under one roof for a while. Conditions were crammed and dire. Three generations of the family had to move together to make room for refugees, who brought little or no belongings, only a rucksack or a suitcase, if they were lucky. The city was destroyed like any other German town and to survive amongst the ruins was a daily challenge.

It was the US army, which first entered Erfurt. After they captured the town all the inhabitants were ordered to leave for twenty-four hours, so that the soldiers could search and pillage without interference and the army could confiscate the buildings they needed for their purposes.

When my family eventually was allowed to return from the fields and forests where they had hidden for those anxious hours, they found that all their valuables had gone. However, the soldiers had filled the cradle of my one-year old cousin Goetz-Olaf with lots of sweets.

But the Americans did not stay long. In the treaty of Yalta 1945 negotiated by Stalin, Roosevelt and Churchill, the Big Three had agreed on how to split up Germany. Thuringia was supposed to end up under Soviet control. Therefore, the American Army left and the Russian Army moved in. Years of Nazi propaganda and the way the Russians had fought their war meant that the defeated were extremely fearful of this move and anxious about the future. Consequently, many people tried to escape to the western zones, which were occupied by the USA, Britain or France.

My mother had another reason for considering moving on. My father's family has its' roots in Frankfurt am Main, which lay in the American zone. It was expected that if he survived the Russian POW camp he would eventually be released there. So, with the help of my father's relatives, she fled again, this time to Frankfurt where she moved in with her mother-in-law, my "Oma", hoping and longing for my father to come back.

My grandfather also survived. He eventually arrived in Erfurt. My grandparents left Hermann's house, to allow more space for other family members, and moved into a flat just around the corner. As it was normal then they did not have the flat to themselves. In the middle of all this destruction everyone in Germany, in all zones of occupation, was allowed only so much space and had to make room for bombed-outs and refugees. So, my grandparents had one room and had to share the kitchen and the bathroom with other families.

3. With us were born two German states

Ute was born in May 1949 in Erfurt. In April 1950 I arrived to the delight of my parents, the "Friedenskindchen" (child of peace), they had longed for. Although Ute and I were close in age and had so much in common, it was by chance that we had landed on different sides of the gap, which, for most of our lives, seemed totally unbridgeable.

Both superpowers, the USA and the Soviet Union, were determined to make their part of Germany a buffer zone as well as a showcase for their respective systems, and on each side, they found enough politicians that were happy to follow suit.

The Bundesrepublik Deutschland (Federal Republic Germany) was established on 23.5.1949 (actually five days after Ute's birthday) in the area that was previously occupied by USA, Britain and France. The Deutsche Demokratische Republik (German Democratic Republic), the area under Soviet occupation, followed on the 7.10.1949. Ute still jokes that as neither she nor her husband was born in the DDR, the state had no right to claim them as loyal subjects.

Until the building of the Wall in 1961, one could still travel between the different zones, despite lots of bureaucratic and other obstacles. So, my parents and I went to Erfurt regularly. For my grandparents it was much more difficult to visit us in Frankfurt. One of the many hurdles was that from 1948 both zones had their own currency, and while the Deutsche

Mark was freely convertible, the Mark (later Mark der DDR) was not. So, if people from East Germany wished to travel, they faced the added difficulty of travelling without means.

In Erfurt I stayed with my grandparents, sometimes with my parents and sometimes on my own. They still shared the flat with other people, and it must have been fairly crowded. But I never thought about it, because I did not know any better. In Frankfurt too, we had to share our flat with other people, my grandmother had one room and we, the young family, had another, until a few years later, when I already could walk and talk, we gained access to some extra space. Ours was the bathroom which doubled as a kitchen, while another family had the use of the proper kitchen, where on Saturday evening they filled a basin for their weekly bath.

For me that was how things were. My generation grew up in cities which still lay in ruins. It was our playground. We had no inkling how much it must have hurt the adults who remembered their surroundings un-destroyed as they were before the war. Only later did I start to reflect on how difficult it must have been for the adults who had been accustomed to living in their own houses with all amenities. Only then did I understand that a certain abruptness in the behaviour of my grandparents might have resulted from their grief and shock at their situation as refugees who had lost everything and in their time of life had to start once more.

Being in Erfurt I spent a lot of time at Hermann's house playing with Ute. Three generations still lived there: Hermann and his wife, Gerti and her husband and of course Ute. If I remember correctly, they also had to take in lodgers. So, space must have been fairly limited as well, but the house seemed large in comparison and they had a garden which was my delight.

In Frankfurt we lived in a block of flats on a main street with lots of traffic. So, children were not allowed to play in front of the house. Behind the house there was a bleak courtyard adjacent to a small strip of grass which was reserved for drying laundry and again strictly out of bounds for us. A proper garden to play in was a paradise, which always belonged to other people and which I sometimes admired through a fence.

The traces of the war were still very visible. When I was a toddler, a large area of Frankfurt was off limits for Germans and fenced off with a barbed wire. It was where American families, related to Army personal, were housed. Like an island of affluence within a sea of destruction, they had their own infrastructure which was superior to ours in every respect. When the barbed wire eventually came down, we were allowed the use of the American play-grounds near-by. To us children it seemed like a dream with all those wonderful swings, see-saws and roundabouts. I still remember my first sip of Coca Cola, when I was about two years old. Not looking where I was going, I had run into a swing and hurt my head badly. I was placed on the floor of the American kindergarten where that strange and tempting drink was poured into my mouth to revive me.

But let us return to Erfurt. Playing with Ute was fine. We were both single children. However, circumstances hardly allowed to call us spoiled. If we ever found it difficult to share fairly, it was more because lacking siblings we were not accustomed to share at all. I can't remember that we argued, but sometimes it got to me when she referred to her seniority and insisted that she should have the larger of the dolls and the larger of the basins in which we bathed those dolls. She was older, that was true, but already then, I was taller. Actually, it is the same today: I am still taller and, in so far as she is my sibling, she is definitely my OLDER sister.

Erfurt is a wonderful medieval town which contains the only bridge north of the Alps with buildings still on it. The town is deeply steeped in the history of the Reformation and has associations with Johann Sebastian Bach and his family. In the 1950s the town must have shown the same traces of the war as Frankfurt did. But for us children ruins were nothing to get excited about. What sticks in my memory was that the structure of the medieval town was still detectable and that some landmarks were less destroyed than others. There was the main square, the mighty cathedral side by side with another church on the cathedral hill. Those images have stayed with me all my life. But more than important buildings I remember small things, like the smell of a brewery nearby which filled the rooms when the wind blew from the east. I also remember the permanent soot and smell of coal fires. They used another coal than we used in Frankfurt, and that special smell for me is inseparably connected to my impressions of Erfurt at that time.

The town had always been famous for its flowers. Cultivation of new varieties was one of the regional industries. A wide area around an old tower called Cyriaksburg hence was designated as a permanent international exhibition of garden designs and flowers. This was a regular destination for family outings on Sunday afternoons as it was a real oasis and had a wonderful play-ground.

My grandfather who was then far beyond the age of retiring still worked as not only was his pension minimal, but with so many war deaths every hand was needed. I remember him guarding the gates of a factory. My grandmother and I went there every day to bring him a hot lunch. I believe that for quite a while the old people hoped that their situation as refugees would be temporary and that one day they would be able to return to their home in Silesia. Eventually it was confirmed that their house in Breslau had been totally destroyed, and it became obvious that Silesia was now part of a new Poland which had no interest in keeping or calling back their German population.

In 1960, after my grandmother's health had declined dramatically, my grandparents eventually decided to migrate from East to West Germany to be closer to their daughter, my mother. Migration was legally possible for those over sixty-five. Although the DDR tried to keep younger and fitter people for the sake of their economic development - and to keep them by all means - they were not unwilling to rid themselves of the elderly or infirm, those who would no longer be productive. People like my grandparents could apply for a permit to migrate which eventually was guaranteed after a lengthy and nerve-killing process.

Meanwhile our situation in Frankfurt had mightily improved. In 1956 we eventually found the means to leave our overcrowded and noisy flat. My "Oma" and my father had received some compensation as victims of the Nazi regime. With that lump sum they were able to put down a deposit for an end-of-terrace house surrounded by a small garden on three sides. When we moved in, it seemed to us like a veritable palace. In hindsight, compared to today's standards, one would call it rather tiny. However, for the first time in my life I had my own room and I felt like a princess when I enjoyed the enormity and the comfort of my first (nearly) grown-up bed.

Unfortunately, when my grandparents arrived in West Germany, they had to move in with us and I had to give up this realm of mine. Of course, the idea had been that they should move into a flat of their own as quickly as possible. But there still remained a painful shortage of accommodation due to the destruction of the war and the millions of refugees from the East who needed space. As a result, for more than two years five adults and one child had to share three not very large bedrooms. Once more I ended up on a mattress in the corner of my parents' room, until my grandparents eventually managed to find a suitable flat and moved out.

A further result of my grandparents leaving the DDR was that the close connection to Ute and her family was interrupted for a while. The adults still exchanged letters and we sent parcels regularly. With the prevailing shortages in the DDR, certain items were very welcome. Those parcels were arguably as important for them as CARE parcels (**C**ooperative for **A**merican **R**emittances in **E**urope, founded in 1945 to relieve post-war suffering in Europe) were for us in the first years after the war. To send parcels was not easy: there were lots of declarations to fill out stating that the parcels contained gifts, no trading goods. The list of contents had to be included threefold. Still it would happen that parcels were refused, confiscated or vanished otherwise on the way.

4. "Nobody is thinking of building a wall."

In 1961 the DDR decided to build the Wall in and around Berlin and to enforce the defences along the border between the DDR and the BRD. From that moment on things went from bad to worse.

Today the Wall exists no more. Some minute parts may be found in hidden corners, but historians started to worry that soon nobody would be able to remember what it really was like and lots of people plead for an adequate memorial.

The physical wall has been demolished, mostly by ordinary people who took hammer and chisel to it in a unique act of individual rebellion and liberation. After what we in Germany call "die Wende" (the Turnaround), everybody wanted a personal piece of history even if it only consisted of a bit of brick and mortar (by the way: we keep ours' on a bookshelf). For many young people today, the Wall is no more than a footnote in a history lesson.

For those who witnessed the Wall being built, it was a nightmare. Only weeks before they started the construction, Walter Ulbricht, the then head of the DDR, surprised the world by stating publicly: "Nobody is thinking of building a wall."

It was the first time that the world had heard somebody mentioning *a Wall*. People thought it weird that this politician was vigorously denying something of which he was not even accused.

15

Town walls had somehow gone out of fashion, since at the end of medieval times people realised that walls could not really protect those who lived within. This wall, however, was not erected to protect a city but to lay siege to one, West-Berlin. And of course, to prevent their own citizens from using the infrastructure of a city, such as streets and trams, underground trains and buses to change from one system into the other.

West-Berlin at that time had around 1.2 million inhabitants. There were urban areas and open country sides, housing areas and industry, trade and agriculture, schools and universities, roads, railways, river harbours and airports. To enclose all this, a wall was built, first brick by brick, later with huge prefabricated concrete slabs. Those who had to work on the construction sites did so guarded by soldiers whose guns were held ready to shoot anyone who might try to flee.

In the first hours and days there were many dramatic and desperate attempts to escape the trap that was quickly closing in on the people. At one point as a first step to stop escapes, barbed wire rolls were lined up as temporary obstacles. One particular photo of a young soldier leaping over theses rolls and, while jumping, throwing away his gun, became one of the most iconic pictures of those days.

Where the line dividing the Soviet and the Western Sectors went through urban areas, it sometimes happened that the front door of a house would be in one sector while the backdoor would be in the other. Such houses were later demolished, but at first the windows and doors leading to the Western Sector were only bricked up. There were pictures of people jumping from higher windows in their desperation to escape to the West, while at the lower windows the work of bricking them up was actually in progress.

For many years a church stood in no-man's land and could be approached neither from the East nor from the West. The DDR border guards used the bell tower to survey the area. Eventually the symbolism was too much even by DDR standards and the church was blown up.

Among the many failed attempts to surmount the Wall none had a stronger impact than that of a young man, Peter Fechtner, in 1962. He was shot and wounded by the DDR border guards and was left to slowly die between the barbed wire fences. In East and West, he could be heard crying for help, but the border guards were under order not to show themselves so that their hide-out would not be identified. The West-Berlin police did not dare to venture into the no-man's land as this could have been understood as aggressive act, and they too could have been shot. It took more than an hour before the official rescue team of the DDR army arrived. They then really tried their best to help. They even asked for and received a first-aid-kid from the West-Berlin police, although by doing so they placed themselves in a dangerous position. But it was all in vain. By the time Peter Fechtner was brought out he had bled to death.

For our family the encapsulation of the DDR meant that contacts became even more difficult. The Wall was not only a physical obstacle, the government of the DDR and the ruling party did their utmost to cut off whatever connections still existed on every level. There was no way to leave the DDR legally, except for a handful of chosen people who were kept under severe observation while being abroad. However, pensioners still could get permission to travel. They were no longer productive and if they choose not to return the state at least could save pensions and healthcare costs.

5. From pen-pals to best of friends

I think it must have been around 1963 or 1964, when Ute and I started to exchange letters. We were thirteen or fourteen years old. I can't remember how our relationship was rekindled; probably it was through her grandfather Hermann, who was still allowed to visit his brother Karl from time to time. It may have been that what he told me about Ute sparked my curiosity.

Equally it is possible that I was slightly influenced by the constant reminder in West Germany about how important it was to keep in touch with "our brothers and sisters" in the East. Western propaganda was no less virulent as that of the other side and used all kind of gestures and symbols to keep their message alive. There were special street signs telling you how far it was to East German towns. Our National Holiday was the 17th of June, the day in 1953, when an attempt to revolt in East Germany was decapitated by Soviet tanks. For many years on this and other days West Germans were called upon to put candles in the windows to demonstrate how much they cared about those behind the "Iron Curtain".

In our letters Ute and I did not discuss politics, at least not openly. We were teenagers and other things were much more important. What we looked like, trouble in school or at home, crushes on movie or pop stars and eventually on boys. Pretty soon we realised that although we seemed to speak the same language there were lots of things in our respective environment that were totally unknown or even alien to the other. As if we came from different planets we had to slowly inform each other about how we lived and which forces influenced our lives beyond our parents. Such we had to enter the mine field of politics in the widest sense of the word. That was tricky, as judgements could be hardly avoided, still none wanted to hurt the other.

The different political and social systems we lived in meant that new words or abbreviations had appeared or well-known words had developed new meanings. A very banal example: to call somebody a "Communist" in West Germany was a terrible insult, whereas in the DDR of course it was the highest praise. We had to learn that one term, absolutely normal for one of us, might be anathema or simply unknown to the other.

I was never very fond of school because I experienced it as rather authoritarian. The majority of our teachers had experienced their own education during the Nazi time. There were even some known ex-Nazis among them, although they were fairly restricted in what they were allowed to teach. Many found it a challenge to open up to discussions and first and foremost demanded quiet obedience. Pupils still got marks then for behaviour, diligence, tidiness and attention.

But that was nothing in comparison with Ute's experiences. When her teachers entered a classroom, the pupils had to stand to attention like little soldiers and had to answer the teacher's formal greeting by shouting slogans in unison. "Discuss!" meant that pupils had to repeat word by word political slogans and then make suggestions how best to fulfil the aim of the party. Even small trespasses were dealt with as if they were political crimes and often the whole family would be afflicted by it.

In the DDR life from a very young age was militarised. Children and teenagers were organised in what was called "Freie Deutsche Jugend" (Liberated German Youth), shortened FDJ, with uniforms and military rituals. If a youngster refused to join, he or she could be sure that admittance to higher education would be blocked and that other disagreeable things would most certainly follow.

And there were more organisations with deceivingly innocent titles. One was "Gesellschaft für Sport und Technik" (Society for Sport and Technique) shortened to GST. This organisation was responsible for military training at all levels of society outside of the regular forces. Every factory for example had its own "Betriebskampfgruppe" (Factory's Battle Group) where workers were regularly trained in the use of weapons. Recruitment to the GST started in school and pupils were attracted by the promise that they would handle real guns. Active members of the GST who promised to join the regular forces later on to become officers could be certain to obtain excellent school marks.

Despite the terrible experiences of the Second World War both states, under the supervision of their occupying forces, had begun to re-arm and to join respective military pacts. In the BRD this happened after an intensive and antagonistic public debate. Even after the decision was taken, the general public mood was such that the newly recruited soldiers were advised not to wear uniforms outside their barracks to not provoke public anger.

To learn from Ute that in East Germany even children were already trained to handle weapons for me was hard to digest. That together with the permanent stream of brain-washing slogans was supposed to prepare them to fight against their enemies. That would be us, me!

My parents had brought me up with abhorrence against war and every kind of militarism. I remember the discussions we had when my father found it terribly difficult to accept that at four-teen I wanted to join the Girl Guides. He simply did not wish to see his daughter in a uniform. Although I eventually joined what was an absolutely civil and un-authoritarian group, I could see his point and avoided parading my gear in front of him.

Through Ute I learned about an education system which seemed to use similar methods and symbols as the Nazis did in their education, and I was deeply shocked. For Ute this was her normal life and she could not afford to despise it as much as I did, because she had to function within this world.

Often it was not easy. But all in all, we were fairly successful in understanding each other. Very soon our exchange of letters became quite intensive. Of course, we wished to meet and to spend some time together. The only way to achieve this was for me to travel to Erfurt during my school holidays.

6. Crossing-over

As a West German you were allowed a single entrance per year with a maximum stay of four weeks. To obtain a permit to enter the DDR temporarily my relatives had to apply to their town's authorities giving lots of details about the visiting person. But permission was given only for next of kin. My connection to Hermann's family was not immediate enough to meet the requirements. Then Ute's mother Gerti declared me to be her niece which, although not strictly true, was eventually accepted. So, after many weeks of tension the permission was eventually given and I could board the train to Erfurt.

The border controls were heavy handed. It took about two hours for the train to be searched from top to bottom, the papers of the travellers checked and individual passengers questioned, who had drawn the attention of the guards. On leaving the DDR border control was even more thorough, as then they searched for potential refugees in each and every corner of the train and ensured that every passport holder was the very person indicated.

In the first years, whenever I crossed the border, one of the main duties of the customs officers was to prevent the smuggling of DDR money into the country. The official exchange rate was set by the DDR and it was utterly absurd. It did not reflect at all what one could buy with the currency. In West Germany one could get DDR money for a fraction of the official exchange rate. As there was no official transfer of money it might have been one of the weapons of the Cold War to undermine the economy of the DDR.

On one occasion I witnessed a man being caught in the act of smuggling money and being arrested. It was eerie as the custom's officers seemed to know exactly what to look for. The normal control had already gone through, when suddenly these policemen entered and went straight for this man. They asked him to hand over his coat and there they found a bundle of notes hidden in the lining. The rest of us fell absolutely silent, shell-shocked. So was the culprit. He offered no excuse and did not show the smallest intention to resist when he was taken away.

Eventually the train moved on. No one spoke a word until we arrived in Erfurt two hours later. I guess there could have been someone in the compartment who had watched something and informed on that poor chap. If we had a snitch among us, he would still be present. Perhaps the others had the same inkling because nobody dared to give a commentary afterwards.

We arrived in Erfurt. Here I was, back for the first time, on the platform. I saw two females coming towards me. First, I did not recognize them, having seen them for the last time when I was about eight or nine. But then I saw that they were followed by the very familiar figure of Uncle Hermann, so I was sure that must be them! Uncle Hermann was always short and stocky. Ute's mother Gerti was as round as she was tiny, Ute was already much taller than her, but I towered over them all.

My size was not the only thing that always attracted the curiosity of those around us. West German visitors were not an everyday occurrence and one was easily spotted by their differences in appearance and dialect. In the first few hours the dialect my relatives spoke was hard to come to terms with. I had loved Ute for the thoughts she expressed in her letters. To hear the same thoughts in the local slang first gave me the creeps.

The main reason was probably that West German media permanently bedevilled or ridiculed this dialect as the language of those in power "over there". As the DDR rulers were painted in hellish colours of course one developed a prejudice against their voices and their way of speaking.

But of course, once I overcame those prejudices I realised that like any other dialect this one had its own charm and virtues. Today as people move around freely in all parts of Germany this or any other dialect would no longer attract any surprise or attention.

The family home was the same as ever, although the layout of the rooms had changed again. Ute has never moved in all her life and still lives there today. But the house was always altered according to family needs with walls coming down or being erected, doors opened or bricked up, and people moving from room to room.

After each arrival in Erfurt I had to report to the police within twenty-four hours. The same had to be done again before I left the country. I was not keen on the feeling of standing in front of the full might of the law. The whole scenario was set so that one could hardly avoid feeling very small and very guilty. Respect bordering on blind obedience towards uniforms and authorities was still expected when one stood in line and when one was questioned. Eventually they condescended to stamp my permit.

They cared a lot for traditions in the DDR and not all of them were recommendable. There are a few nations whose citizen can be really nice if you meet them individually. That is until you put them into a uniform and give them if only the minutest power. Then they readily turn into brainless monsters. Unfortunately, we have had enough of this during the last hundred years of German history.

7. Going out shopping

I became quickly aware of the almost complete absence of commercial advertisements which were replaced by an overwhelming presence of political propaganda. Red banners carrying encouraging slogans were everywhere, some almost poetic in their choice of words and in their absurdity. "Socialism will win, because it is right!", "To learn from the Soviet Union, means to learn how to win!", "All our strength for the next Party conference". 'Onwards' was an extremely important term that reappeared constantly.

For Ute this was her normal environment. She assured me that they hardly registered it any longer. In my world I probably would have taken the colourful pictures on placards selling soap to the public for granted and would not have wasted a second thought on them. That was true in a manner of speaking; the small difference being that one could buy or not buy the soap, while the victorious Soviet Union could do little to keep your body clean.

To imitate the Soviet example had to be taken literally. Word by word translation of Russian slogans added a certain unintended humour to public communications. The naming of streets and buildings strictly following Russian fashion always sounded a bit pompous. A crude example (as translations are always difficult) could be that a building which otherwise would be a Youth Centre (Jugendzentrum) here became "The House of the Youth" (Haus der Jugend). A street name to celebrate women could be: "Street of the 8th of March", a working men's club would be "Club for the Working Men".

Already in the sixties there were differences between what you could purchase here and there. But it was not yet as extreme as it would be in later years. After the erecting of the Wall and the closing-down of other escape routes East Germans had their own smaller version of a "Wirtschaftswunder", (miracle of an economic recovery). Perhaps it happened because skilled workers could no longer leave the country for the golden troughs of the West, so production improved. Or the government understood that they had to allow more private consumption in order to keep their citizens, if not satisfied, then at least quiet. Therefore, they spent more money on imports and allowed more retail goods to be produced.

So far as standards of living were concerned I felt quite at home. In Frankfurt, far from being well off, my family just got by. Of course, we could not afford all we might have wanted. Thus, I was quite happy with what I was offered in Erfurt although I might have occasionally put my foot in with my relatives by quite innocently mentioning things we in the West were accustomed to and which they would be never able to obtain.

On one occasion, I was served fresh asparagus (of which I was never a big fan). Everybody was watching while I tried to be polite and eat what was put on my plate without showing my distaste. My effort was greeted with the eager question of how I liked them, and, incurably honest, I answered that among vegetables this was not necessarily my favourite.

The reaction was a general indignation. How could I call a delicacy like asparagus 'a vegetable'? Did I know what kind of an uphill struggle it had taken to obtain those few fresh asparagus stalks? It was obviously that family and friends had worked so hard on all their connections in order to please me and in the end, I was nothing but an ungrateful spoilt Western brat.

Prices in the DDR were fixed nationally according to political objectives rather than related to the cost of production. Rent and basic food was always extremely cheap in comparison to any market economy. So was public transport. Tramways cost only a few Pfennige. After you entered a tram you had to throw your pennies into a machine which was no more than a money box. Next you pulled a trigger and received your ticket. It would have been easy to cheat because there was no mechanical check as to whether you had thrown in the correct fare. But you were watched all the time by the people around you. They probably would have made you aware very quickly if you had made a mistake.

Thus, I learnt about the power of that public control. Even people who had a travel pass when entering a train would hold it up and to let it be seen by everybody. I wondered what they were doing as there was nobody to control the tickets and asked Ute. Once more it was one of those occasions where we seemed to come from different planets. Ute informed me that if the other passengers could not see that a person boarding had a travel card this person could be thought to be a fare dodger as he had not made use of the ticket dispenser.

"Who cares?" I asked. "As long as they have their travel passes ready should a controller come around?"

"We care." she informed me emphatically.

While everyday goods were cheap, anything considered a luxury was extremely expensive. But prices were not really the problem. In the late sixties and even more so later the average DDR citizen probably had more money than he or she could spend. The problem was that centrally planned production never met with general demand and thus many goods were rationed. For goods like cars, technical equipment, furniture and many others people had to join waiting lists and be patient. For a new *Trabant*, the famous hallmark of DDR car production, waiting times were about ten years. This meant used cars, which could be traded privately, were more expensive than new ones. By word of mouth they were sold on and on, repaired and repaired again, until, out of several damaged bodies and broken engines handicraft enthusiasts built themselves very individual specimens.

With those long waiting times for cars, everybody of the right age applied for a car as soon as they could. Thus, it happened that one family could be waiting for three or four cars to be delivered in due time to different members of the family. Whenever one car was delivered the addressee immediately ordered the next one. So, a family might have driven a new car every second year and by selling off the old one could have made a nice profit.

There was even a trade in orders. You could buy or sell an order for a car. The nearer the date of delivery came, the more valuable the order was. Of course, the buyer paid only for the saved time. He then still had to pay the full price for the new car before it was delivered. All "luxury" goods were paid for in advance or on delivery. There was no system of credits, no "buy now and pay later".

There were always shortages. Many goods were very hard to come by. On occasions when rare offers appeared nevertheless, information about the "what" and "where" were traded through the same unofficial channels. On one occasion many years later, Ute heard through the grapevine that carpets would be sold at a certain shop. She knew somebody who knew somebody and so one morning, hours before the shop opened officially, we joined the crowd. Indeed, they had a few rolls of carpet and the shop was already full with people placing their orders.

Luckily Ute got what she wanted and we went home elated. Later that day Ute remembered that she wanted to ask something about the cleaning of the new carpet, and so we returned to the shop. That was during the normal opening hours. The shop was empty. There were no carpets left and consequently there were no customers. The sales personnel had a nice chat and it took them a while to realise that we had a request they could indeed satisfy.

There was never a shortage of the most basic food but for everything else, ruled by long-term planning, only so was much produced or imported. Once it was sold that was it for a long time. Those permanent gaps on the shelves led to habits which seemed totally normal to Ute and utterly strange to me. She never went out without an extra bag in case she saw something that was not always available. When, while strolling around, we came upon some exceptional offer, she bought it whether she needed it or not just because it was there. I remember on one occasion I did my best to convince her that flip-flops we discovered following a long queue of excited buyers were simply ugly and that she should not spend money on them. She could not but agree, especially concerning the aesthetical value of those shoes, but she was nearly in tears when I pulled her away. She implored me again and again that next summer when those flip-flops might come in handy and might be the height of fashion she would not be able to purchase them anymore.

One would automatically join a queue, even without knowing what would be on offer when one reached the counter, just in case. As everybody reacted in that way, it was small wonder that everything out of the ordinary sold out on the spot. Whether you needed a particular object or could even use it was of no consequence because those things you could still exchange for something you would need indeed. A lively secondary economy existed on the basis of those exchanges. Officially, the government tried to clamp down on this shady trading; but secretly they knew that without it the whole system would have broken down much sooner.

There were a lot of jokes in circulation about this and other aspects of life within the 'Real Existing Socialism' as it was called. In all repressive systems humour functions a kind of safety valve. However, everyone who told a joke or a funny anecdote knew that there could be trouble if the wrong people overheard it and reported the conversation.

Here is one typical joke:

Man to shop assistant: "You wouldn't have tomatoes by any chance, would you?"

Shop assistant: "You have to ask in the shop next door. They don't have tomatoes. In this shop, we don't have cucumber."

And yet all the humour in the world helped little with coping with all the daily shortages. A good part of every family conversation revolved around tracing rare goods and organising necessary supply. Sources were discussed and weighted for their reliability. What could or should be put up as an offer? Often long chains were formed where one traded one good against another only because this particular good would open the door to the eventual supplier of the desired item.

In my world, in Frankfurt, everything one could possibly dream of was of course on offer. There was only the minor problem of the necessary cash. In my family we spent the same amount of time in discussing how we could earn and save enough money, not only to pay the bills at the end of the months, which was difficult enough, but to obtain that little bit extra we longed for. As my parents found it difficult to provide me with pocket money, I started to earn my own money very early and most of what I owned I had paid for myself.

Ute understood my situation perfectly well and never nagged me for anything. But there were occasions when it was not easy to make other friends understand that I could not help them or bring them presents. I simply could not afford it. They knew what was on offer in the West. They saw it on television. Why then was I so unfriendly as not to take that little bit of trouble and bring them the things they so much desired?

8. Tell me what program you watch!

Television had a lot to answer for. In the DDR nearly everybody watched West German television. All they had to do was to move the aerial a bit and there it was: the sounds and pictures of the golden West. Of course, the impression they got was rose-tinted. There were all the colourful advertisements showing happy parents with children around the family table enjoying a particular brand of margarine. Dirt disappeared magically. Nature looked beautiful, while politicians looked responsible. Even when social problems were addressed there always seemed to be a solution. At the end of the overwhelming majority of thrillers or detective stories the inspector while pointing at the evildoer stated: "It was you! Take him away!" and that was it.

The DDR authorities would have loved to be rid of this window into another world, but somehow, they did not dare to suppress it totally. Rather they tried to win their audience by competition. East German television schedule was often timed so that attractive shows or sport-events ran parallel to popular West German programs.

In East and West, they transmitted programs specially dealing with the other side. A famous show in the DDR was "Der schwarze Kanal", "the black channel" being the West German TV station of course. They took sequences from the two West German stations and put them together to paint a picture of a deeply unjust and decadent society on the brink of chaos and murder.

On West German TV a "ZDF (Zweites Deutsches Fernsehen = Second German Channel) Magazin" answered weekly by describing the DDR as a gigantic prison where millions of incarcerated sighed under Stalin's knout. The problem was that not everything was an obvious lie, but even truths can be twisted to the point that people simply stop listening. This was the Cold War and mass-communications, in the form of TV and Radio, was one of the many battlefields.

Geographically there was only one area of the DDR where West German programs were totally out of reach. This was jokingly called 'The Valleys of the Innocent', because the people there did not enjoy the same kind of antidote against the messages of their own media and therefore were thought to be less critical. For them the "Black Channel" was one of the few occasions where they could take a – if twisted – look into what was going on in West Germany.

Of course, there were no TV journals covering West German programs published or sold in East Germany. To help out there was a special TV broadcast on Sunday morning giving detailed information of the schedule for the coming week. Each Sunday morning Ute had to sit down and to copy the whole TV programme from the screen. This was a sacrosanct moment which was not to be disrupted at any cost. Everybody had to shut up so that Ute could concentrate. No appointment would be made and visitors were not welcome for this hour.

Without Ute's efforts the family would have missed out on what was considered a very important source of information. And so, it might have been in many families in the DDR. But whenever the television set was switched off, it was first set back to the East German Channel just in case somebody came and checked.

It was an open secret. Once Ute and I visited a funfair. There was a raffle draw. The caller used the very same words that were used in the West German TV lottery to announce the winning numbers. His audience thought it hilarious and applauded him vividly. Each and everyone understood the hint immediately and appreciated the courage of the caller to hint at the possibility that he might be breaking the law like everybody else.

On a more sinister note I learned from Ute that schools would gather information about the TV watching habits of pupils and their parents. Teachers had to ask first formers to watch out whether the clock on the TV screen had points or lines for the minutes. They used the youngest pupils because they were still innocent enough not to realise that by doing this homework they divulged their family's political orientation.

9. Girls will be girls

Ute and I were teenagers then and of course we were interested in fashion, music and everything teenagers would indulge in. With international media which are transporting new must-haves all over the globe, it may seem a strange idea but to my strongest belief fashion was and still is a fairly regional affair. Since 1965 I regularly spent part of my holidays in London, which was then the European capital of fashion and music. Music travelled fast but as far as clothes went I always felt that we in West Germany were about a year or two behind the latest London craze. Between West and East Germany there was another time lag. Ute and her friends looked at what I wore with awe and abhorrence. Most of the times they then went for the same stuff about a year later.

But this was not the only difference between Ute and me. Whatever she wore she always took some pride in good quality and perfection. She enjoyed knitting and was very talented in copying all kinds of pattern. When from time to time she could lay her hands on some suitable fabric she had a special friend who would create something for her out of a fashion magazine.

I on the other hand bought most of my clothes second hand, the older the merrier. I was more interested in looking a bit eccentric than being perfectly styled. I realised that whatever I spent my money on in a month or so it would be out of fashion again.

So, I became a sales-and-reduced-junkie and still have relapses regularly.

Still today Ute reminds me of "that wonderful skirt" I very proudly had written to her about, the "mother" of all skirts – and not expensive at all. When I arrived in Erfurt it turned out to be a long old woolly piece of unclear but dark colours which she would have thrown out as quickly as possible if only I had allowed her to do so. With this skirt I wore an equally old long fur coat which had lost most of its hair and smelled a bit strong. I was the incarnation of "Love and Peace" and my East German friends pretended not to know me when we hit the town.

In the late sixties and the early seventies, I most certainly was of the hippie tribe while Ute already was en route to becoming a lady. Her most prevailing memory of me at that time is:

"You always wanted to sit and sleep on the floor. We could hardly get you to use a proper chair or a bed."

Ute's parents were even more conservative and made no secret of their disapproval, so we tried to get away as much as possible. Unfortunately, in Erfurt there was not much one could go out to. The town centre was not really an inviting area to hang out. Of course, there were a few beautiful old buildings, but not all the damage from the war was dealt with, and most of the city was depressingly run down. It was the same in Frankfurt, although there might have been a difference in the speed of reconstruction. However, this reconstruction was carried out similarly here and there: functional, horrible and heartless.

There were hardly any coffee houses, pubs or restaurants. Those that existed were large and practical. They were supposed to feed the working masses not to amuse them. You had to queue for an eternity and even when you eventually got a place you were not encouraged to overstay your welcome. One had to make room for the next waiting customer as soon as possible. Therefore, comfort or considerate service was not part of the deal.

In the entertainment business as in other areas, private initiative would not have been welcome at all. The state just about tolerated private enterprises such as craftsmen if they had existed before the DDR was founded, although their trade was heavily restricted. But to start up a new business was totally out of question. Thus, small very individual places for different tastes and income, which are so important in creating a charming atmosphere in a city, were virtually unknown.

The same was true for "Discos" or "Clubs". They did not exist. Young people in the DDR had other, less decadent ways to amuse themselves, politicians would tell you. The same politician would eagerly deny that misuse of alcohol or drugs existed in their perfect society or that teenager could show behavioural deviations.

Of course, the authorities were aware that they had to allow some room for young people to burn off energies, so under strict control they turned public buildings into dance halls for an evening. And there we went.

It was fun. The band copied international charts and the music was absolutely danceable. Prices were comparatively low and while in a Frankfurt disco I had to survive the night on one coke with rum, for the same amount of money I could get nicely drunk in Erfurt.

I was not the only one. A lot of people drank a lot on these occasions, I was quite amazed to realise.

I have a hazy memory of three of us wandering home one night because the tram had already stopped running. The third person being one of Ute's male friends, we took turns to snog on every park bench we passed. Discreetly we threw up behind bushes. I don't think our behaviour that night could be recommended by any standard not to mention the 'rounded socialistic personality'!

From time to time we went to the cinema. Of course, the absolute majority of movies released were produced either in the DDR or in one of the socialistic "brother" states. Often the message was so blunt and obvious that to avoid it was arguably the best you could do. But there were exceptions. As in literature from time to time individuals dared to depart from the party line and present a subtle reflection on the realities of life. Some Russian movies were beautifully poetical with slowly moving camera shots and with impressive landscapes in the background. Very early on, France had developed special relations with many countries in Eastern Europe, so some French movies reached the DDR cinemas. Most of these films, however, were comedies which avoided any open commentary on political or social themes, although they allowed the cinema audience a glimpse into French life, which turned a not altogether real France into a kind of dreamland for many people.

Whenever a Hollywood movie made it into DDR cinemas it was quite a sensation. Most vividly I remember us watching the famous movie *Spartacus*, starring Kirk Douglas. When we left the cinema Ute suddenly burst out that this was how they felt. I never found out whether she meant it was the way she personally felt under the DDR regime or whether she saw herself as part of the suppressed working class in a worldwide struggle against capitalists and imperialists as her education would have suggested.

Perhaps it was a strange kind of consideration that sometimes made me shrink back from putting her on the spot about what she really thought and felt. It was easy for me to be critical with what went on around me. After a few weeks I would be allowed to leave the DDR again. She could not leave. Somehow, she had to make her own peace with her circumstances. If that included turning a blind eye in some cases I could not blame her.

We did share many political and social attitudes and some of those did not even contradict the values the socialist countries stood for. International solidarity was very important to both of us. We both wanted the Americans out of Vietnam and thought with horror of what was happening in Latin America and other parts of the world where US imperialistic interests ruled mercilessly.

Though we both were politically interested we shared a lot of other interests as well. At certain times we clung to the radio to listen to the same music on the same (Western) radio stations' weekly hit programs. In West Germany we taped music from the radio because it was so much cheaper than buying records. In the East, where this outlandish music was not welcome and international pop records were not available, to tape from the radio was the only possible way to possess and afterwards to trade those highly cherished songs. A united nation of teenagers sat beside the radio ready to push the start button and to explode once more with rage if the announcer dared to babble over the beginning or the end of a hit.

10. Getting into trouble

The East German authorities were obviously worried by the influence of international pop culture on their youth but wise enough not to suppress it completely. According to the saying: 'if you can't beat them, join them', they later allowed their own version of pop music and a few good bands appeared on the scene. As with fashion there always was a slight delay. A new craze was first denounced and those who followed it or imitated the band's outfits faced serious trouble. When too many people wore the same kind of fashion and listened to the same music they tried to add to it a special socialist twist and allowed it under controlled circumstances. Again, besides the officially approved offers there was a lively black market for smuggled records or tapes. I probably was a coward, but I never tried to smuggle anything forbidden into the DDR. Or, to put it more positively, if I had to get into trouble it had to be for the right reasons.

Actually, I got myself into trouble. During one of my first stays in Erfurt West German visitors were invited – read: ordered – to attend a meeting where for two hours officials preached us their version of the political and social realities in both German states. About fifty West Germans were present, mostly elderly and subdued. Nobody dared to argue. They just sat there and let it all wash over them, anxious not to displease the might of the state.

I could not have been much older than fourteen but already I detested being intimidated so at the first moment of silence I started to ask questions. First, they tried to argue with me, but I was quite persistent. Eventually the speaker lost his nerve and exploded. That it was easy for me to be a smartarse here, he shouted, and that I should go back to my own side and ask probing questions there. With as much dignity as I could muster, I got up, told him that the very idea I would not dare to speak up in any situation where I was being forced to listen to a lot of rubbish was laughable, and left the meeting. Two or three others followed me. The rest stayed put.

When I came back to my relatives and told them what had happened I could sense their agitation. They were anxious as to what the reaction would be. Who would have to bear the brunt of my misbehaviour? That I told them I did nothing wrong did not help very much. I realised how much an arbitrary use of power could shift the understanding of right or wrong. The question was no longer: do you obey the law, but: do you please those in power.

Fortunately, none of my relatives got into trouble because of this event. The next year I was allowed to re-enter the DDR as usual. However, I was never again invited to such a meeting. Furthermore, from what I heard these invitations stopped altogether. There must have been more visitors like me who had given the speakers a hard time. The organizers perhaps realised that if they regularly lost the argument in defending the indefensible it did not help to prove the superiority of their political system.

In one way I broke the law on every visit. The permit to temporarily stay was valid for only one district. Legally I was not allowed to leave Erfurt at all. But with both our grandfathers originating from Thuringia we had more relatives in the area. In order to see them I should have applied for further permits and reported to the respective local authorities. But once I had complied with the basic registration in Erfurt we never bothered and went around without ever being challenged.

11. Weimar, Eisenach and Buchenwald – the different faces of Germany's history

It was not only relatives I wanted to visit. There are many places in the vicinity which deserve to be mentioned. Only a few miles away is Weimar, which played an important role in Germany's cultural and political history. Johann Wolfgang von Goethe was a leading statesman there and while he lived and after his decease his personality attracted many other remarkable people. After the First World War Weimar was the place where the new and democratic constitution of the first republic was laid down and thus gave its name to the whole epoch.

For me, Weimar was particularly interesting because of a further family connection. One of the important institutions connected to the town was the *Bauhaus.* It was a place where after the First World War and in consequence of revolutionary attempts in Germany important artists tried to liberate *ART* from traditionalism and turn it practical. One main aim was to bring together art and crafts. As a school it was especially influential in modern architecture and design. Many famous painters and sculptors were professors or students there.

The oldest brother of my 'Oma', Ludwig Hirschfeld-Mack, entered the Bauhaus 1919 as an apprentice and was the first to rise through the ranks to become a professor of art himself. At that time the Bauhaus was situated in Weimar and so the exhibition which presented its history and artefacts always had a profound personal meaning for me.

Ludwig Hirschfeld-Mack's biography reflects a particular aspect of the darkest and most traumatic part of German history; this is why I would like to give you a short summary.

After Hitler came to power there was more than one reason to force my great-uncle into exile. Apart from his Jewish background, his art represented everything the Nazis detested. And he had become a Quaker, a convinced and active pacifist, as a result of what he had witnessed during the First World War, in which he had served as a highly decorated German officer.

In 1936 together with his eldest daughter he fled to Britain where he found employment as an art teacher. When war was declared he was arrested as were all German men. It made no difference whether they were representatives of the Nazi regime caught by the events, or Jewish or political refugees in deadly fear of the "Third Reich", all German men and women were considered 'enemy aliens'.

Ludwig was deported to Australia on an infamous ship, the HMS Dunera. There the internees, who came from different European countries, were badly mistreated and robbed of their last possessions. The captain had informed his crew that they were all Nazis, and that they could do to them what they wanted. Many of the internees were in fact refugees; many came from countries under German occupation and some had even suffered in German concentration camps.

In Australia they were transferred into a prisoner of war camp in the middle of the bush. This camp was remarkable because the prisoners, many of them highly educated or talented, in order to keep themselves occupied during the long years of incarceration, formed their own college and university, where eventually official degree courses could be taken.

After the end of the war Ludwig decided not to return to Europe. He stayed in Australia and there he became an inspirational art teacher. Although in Australia many people remember him, in Europe today he is nearly forgotten, as were so many artists whose biographies had been broken by fascism.

But let us return to the Weimar I knew. Another of my mother's cousins lived there with her husband who very fittingly was an architect and a lecturer in architecture. While Erfurt's old centre is mainly shaped by medieval structures, in Weimar it is the classical period of the late 18th and early 19th century and later *Art Nouveau* and *Arts and Crafts* which predominates the panorama. None of the town's buildings are on a large scale, not even the palaces. Even in its heyday Weimar was no more than the residence of one of the numerous Grand Dukes within the old Empire, whose small realm was furthermore split up over several provinces. This is exactly what makes it so utterly charming and accessible.

One of my favourite places is Castle Belvedere with its surrounding parks, which is an easy stroll from the centre of town. It is tiny, beautiful and typical of the early 18rds. There was always music to be heard from the building and in the park, because it was home of the Weimar Music Academy. Today it is a secondary school which still specialises in musical education.

I have cherished memories of days in the sun. We strolled around the park listening to the music which drifted towards us with the wind. There was a little maze in which to lose yourself was absolute delightful and not frightening at all. We talked about the Classics and about Goethe, who having been born in Frankfurt connected my hometown to Weimar. We would happily indulge in history, pretend we were Goethe's contemporaries, and forget about the present.

Another highlight was the *Wartburg* near Eisenach, a castle on top of a hill, where Luther translated the Bible into German. In doing so he not only laid the foundation for the Reformation but created a basis for a common German language.

We made the pilgrimage to the castle guided by Ute's grandfather Hermann. Of course, we devoutly studied the stain on the wall where, as the legend goes, Luther threw an ink bottle at the devil who tried to tempt him. For a romantic the Wartburg is the ideal of a fortress with its walls seemingly growing out of the rocks on which it was built. From the look-out of the highest tower you can see for miles and miles over a landscape which moulded Prince Albert's picture of natural beauty, a beauty, which he rediscovered in the Scottish Deeside, where Queen Victoria and he eventually built Balmoral Castle.

Thuringia belongs to the heartlands of the Reformation. With places like Wittenberg, where Luther hammered his 95 theses to the cathedral door, to Eisleben, where he was born in 1483 and died in 1546, it was the cradle of Lutheranism which is the prevalent form of Protestantism in Germany.

Even the DDR could not fully deny traditions. Among its historical roots it strongly incorporated the Peasant's Revolt which followed the break with the Catholic Church (1524-1525). This very early cry for freedom from serfdom and freedom of believes first spread like a wildfire. Some of their leaders became legendary. It was so successful that even local noblemen joined it. Against their own material interests, they were affected by the general feeling of euphoria over the new-found freedom of the individual. However, the way things were developing meant that the newly founded church would either be open to any attack from Rome or totally dependent on the grace of the respective rulers. And when those rulers demanded it, Luther publicly denounced and deserted the peasants' cause. Having lost one of its fundaments the revolt degenerated into looting and burning and was eventually defeated cruelly.

Now the heartland of Protestantism was governed by socialists to whom religion was anathema. Nevertheless, there existed a certain collusion between the official church and the state. The people in power realised soon that suppressing the churches would mean to open up one more front, while a conforming church at least would help to keep people quiet. Subtly a battle was going on to turn hearts and minds away from religion. Great efforts were made to replace First Communion or Confirmation by what was called 'Jugendweihe'. It was a designed as a rite of passage, in which fourteen-year olds would publicly promise to be faithful to socialism and to their state. This was normally followed by a family party and lots of presents so that teenagers were not averse to prepare for their Great Day.

Ute could not refuse this promise but she insisted on having her confirmation as well and to have a celebration only after the religious event. As an adult she donated regularly to her local parish and was married in church. This was not the rule with young couples and took some stamina. Although I am not religious at all, I hold Ute in high esteem because she followed her own convictions and refused to submit totally to the desires of the party and the state.

One place I needed to see with my own eyes was the KZ (Konzentrationslager = concentration camp) Buchenwald, half way between Erfurt and Weimar. In the sixties more and more information about the crimes of the Nazis came to light and were intensively discussed. My family background made me want to find out as much as I could about it. However, the emphasis on what were the main features of German fascism was quite different in East and West. While in West Germany the public discussion focused on the enormity of the racial persecutions, the DDR gave priority to the sufferings of the working class and their representatives. Recently, in my hometown Frankfurt a famous court case had shown in gruesome detail the workings of industrial murder in Auschwitz and highlighted the German guilt towards the Jews and other peoples. In East Germany the communist victims of the Third Reich were held in high esteem. Prominent amongst them was Ernst Thälmann, who had been the Chairman of the Communist Party before the Nazis forced the party into illegality, and who was murdered in Buchenwald.

It was a beautiful sunny summer day when I first entered the compound. This made it even worse. Buchenwald was the first KZ I ever saw and somehow all my mental pictures were in black and white, heaps of utter misery under a grey crying sky. The realisation that time never stood still and that the prisoners must have witnessed winters and summers, rain and sunshine, days like this - sunny days - made it much more real and much more gruesome. Did their hopes rise when spring eventually came and frost retreated? It can be so bitterly cold on the top of the Ettersberg! Would they have looked down from the hill to the surrounding country side with its villages and towns? What did they feel when they saw a kind of normal life going on around them and nobody taking notice of what was happening on the hill? Would they have wondered if the world had completely forgotten them? And what about the people who lived nearby? How easy was it to close eyes and ears against what was happening in their vicinity?

Over the main gate the SS had placed these cynical words in wrought iron: "Jedem das Seine" ('Each as he deserves'). The sheer cruelty is untranslatable. It suggests that people were incarcerated here for well-deserved punishment for crimes they had committed. Nothing could be further from the truth.

Buchenwald was not an extermination camp like Auschwitz and other infamous KZs in Poland. Still tens of thousands perished here and their deaths were wanted and welcomed by the system.

When I visited the camp, it was destroyed to a large extent. This was neither due to the fleeing SS nor to the allied armies. Quite the contrary, the occupying forces of the USSR until 1950 continued to use the KZ as a prison camp for Nazis and those they suspected of opposing their regime. The later dismantling had been a decision of the DDR rulers because they planned to convert the whole area into one big shrine for Ernst Thälmann and his fellow comrades who had been murdered here.

We walked the grounds and visited the exhibition in silence. I knew and appreciated that heroic deeds had been done by the inmates who belonged to the communist party. During many years they had kept up a secret organization and thus probably enabled many fellow sufferers not to lose hope and to survive. Still I thought that this insistence on heroes was a strange attempt to make sense of something which is so utterly overwhelming because indeed it does not make sense at all. I wished the nameless tens of thousands that perished would not be forgotten either.

When I talked to Ute afterwards I realised that she was not as aware as I was of the racist aspects of the Nazi regime, while she told me a lot about the persecution of the communists and trade unionists which I had never heard before. We were both amazed how much we had never been told. Aspects of history could so easily be hidden by what seemed to be an agreement not to mention them. It was not forbidden to speak about the Jewish victims in the DDR, as in the BRD it was totally legal to point out the suppression of left-wing parties and organisations during the Nazi time. But it was treated as an afterthought, as it would have interfered with a predominant interpretation of the Third Reich.

In principle we were both sceptical of our respective states and of their ruling ideologies. When we discussed politics, it was not to prove each other wrong. We were critical of many things but we did not follow any party line. We had nothing to defend as neither of us identified totally with the system in which we had grown up. Only on one occasion we had a nasty quarrel, very unlike our usual unbiased discussions. It started as a normal conversation dealing with political matters. But the atmosphere changed. Instead of standing side by side in a manner of speaking, studying a situation from a similar angle and trying to find out what it meant and what it was all about, we suddenly faced each other angrily and ended in exchanging insults. I felt attacked as a person and in my way of living and started to defend a political system I normally would have hardly defended. That I then attacked Ute in the same manner only exacerbated the tension between us. But as quickly as this quarrel erupted it came to a sudden end, when Ute turned around, laughed and admitted that she only had been quoting political slogans she heard every day to test their value against serious opposition.

12. The Swinging Sixties

Between the foundation of the Federal Republic and the late Sixties West Germany was ruled by old men from the CDU/CSU (CDU=Christlich Demokratische Union, CSU=Christlich Soziale Union in Bavaria). The CDU/CSU was an amalgamation of several conservative and catholic parties which had ceased to exist when the Nazis in 1933 forbade all other parties. Amongst its' members were a few who had actively resisted Hitler and suffered for it. But even more had been active Nazis and some even had held high ranks in military or civil organisations of the Third Reich.

Their most popular slogan for general elections was: 'No changes!' which met exactly with the general mood of the population. After the total disaster of the lost war: the deaths, the destruction and the millions of refugees, all that people wanted was a bit of peace and quiet plus the chance to rebuild their own lives. Society was stuffy, morals were prudish and manners were stiff. It was quietly suffocating.

The same was certainly true in East Germany. In 1953 a failed attempt to rebel against the Soviet occupation and the DDR government had shaken the nation. The aftermath of this revolt was cruel and bloody. Certainly, it was one of the triggers for many people to leave East Germany. The possibility to escape was brought to a halt by erecting the Wall. Now the overwhelming majority seemed to have learned to shut up and get on with their lives.

However, by the end of the sixty's things began to change all over the world. The Vietnam War was an international stimulus for protest. Closer to home our generation started to question the silence our parents kept about the crimes of the Third Reich. Everywhere authority was questioned. Music and fashion came together to define our generation as fundamentally divided from our elders.

Between Ute and myself, I was the more rebellious. But of course, for me things were much easier. If my parents had learnt one lesson from the past it was that one had to stay alert constantly and that it was a duty to fight any prejudices and injustices. My father convinced me to read newspapers from an early age and we discussed what was going on incessantly. Both of my parents included me in their decision on their votes as long as I was not allowed to take part in general elections myself. When I started to take part in demonstrations they supported me wholeheartedly and stood by me when I got into trouble at school because of my political engagement.

My father's mother, my beloved 'Oma', had been extremely brave during the Nazi era. She had managed to save her parents from deportation and certain death. But she was the only one to occasionally caution me. It was not because she thought my political beliefs false, she was just afraid that I would attract unwelcome attention. Her rule of survival, which was deeply ingrained, after all she had been through, was that whatever you did, you had to avoid attracting the eye of the authorities. One had to keep up appearance and not let those in power know what one really thought. I did not follow her advice but I appreciated where she came from and thus I understood that Ute and her family probably felt similar. Whatever their convictions they had to remain within the family and for the outside world they had to show something akin to a blank face.

At this time my secondary school was a 'Gymnasium' (grammar school) and took my 'Abitur' (comparable to A-levels) in 1968. Fairly early I choose to read sociology at Frankfurt University which had a few famous sociology and philosophy professors. I had great expectations that through them I would learn to understand how something like the Third Reich could have happened and what the individual could do to stop it ever happening again.

For the longest time of my life that theme kept me firmly in its grip. I wanted to know as much about the "Truth" as it was possible to learn. My very vague picture of the future included that perhaps one day I would have to save the world if that went through as a job description. I was less interested in acquiring a profession or the tricks of one trade. I had no proper concept of a time when my student days would end and a proper employment with a regular income should follow.

Circumstances forced Ute to be much more realistic and down to earth. The DDR, where everything was subjected to central planning, restricted people in their choice of education, professions and employments according to those plans, their social origins and their personal behaviour. Ute was an excellent pupil, but when she had passed what could be compared to GCSEs she was not allowed to go on to do 'Abitur' as her parents were not considered members of the "working-class" and only "working class" children were allowed to proceed to higher education. Her parents were both accountants in a small company and their income was not different from that of average workers in a factory and yet they were called "middle-class". Needless to say, that the children of party cadres were always rated as "working-class" whatever the actual profession of their parents.

Years later Ute's husband Eberhard, a master locksmith with a comparatively high income, was rated "working-class" and their daughter Susanne was allowed to take her 'Abitur' and to go to university.

With her school graduation, the most intellectually challenging profession Ute could aim at was to become a primary school teacher. She registered at a teacher's college in Weimar. So, while I was still at school, she was already a student and I envied her for that. However, the college was organised more like a boarding school and offered little of the freedom one might associate with student life. They had a very strict timetable and hardly any choice in what they could read. Attendance was compulsory and staff had the same kind of authority as school teachers. The cramped accommodation was rather depressing too. Four girls had to share a small room with two sets of bunk beds, one table and four chairs. When I visited I thought that it must be really difficult under those circumstances to concentrate on your revisions.

13. Friends and more

When she was little Ute had a best friend from whom she was truly inseparable. When that friend disappeared literally over night without so much as a good bye, Ute was heartbroken. It was before the Wall, when crossing the border illegally was dangerous but still possible. Her friend's parents were both doctors and hoped that they would find a better life in West Germany. So, they decided to leave in the middle of the night and of course there could be no advance warning and no fare wells.

For a long time, Ute suffered from her loss and in her school days while she was well liked by her mates she never had another close friend. Whenever I visited her it was just the two of us and I can't remember ever having met her schoolmates or others of the same age.

All that changed when Ute started college. From that moment on she did not mind me meeting her co-students and her friends. Then we spent a lot of time in groups. Among her friends I was a bit of a sensation. West Germans without direct relatives never had the chance to visit the DDR and many, who had relatives, still preferred not to do so because they were anxious of what could happen to them. Years of permanent anti-communist propaganda had thus taken its toll. So, it was that many in East Germany never had any personal contact with a West German person.

The permanent propaganda from their side meant that there were some expectations about how such an alien would be and behave. I probably did not altogether fit the picture and after a while any excitement calmed down. Mostly I was treated as a welcome and interesting guest. Perhaps the pedestal I was sometimes placed on was a bit too high for my own good. For a sixteen/seventeen-year-old it was quite flattering to be considered 'interesting', to be questioned and to be listened to.

Amongst Ute's friends there was one who showed a particular interest in me and made me promise to write to him. His name was not Bernhard, but I shall call him so, as he had no chance for a veto against me telling his story. He was attractive in every aspect. Not only was he rather good looking but he was also intelligent and sensible and thought a lot about many things that troubled me as well. So, I headed into another pen pal friendship and while I still was staying with Ute and her family, there was now a second reason to return to Erfurt.

Very soon I thought myself to be in love. You do, you know, when you are sixteen and the situation is as romantic and as dramatic as ours was. Tragically we were separated by forces beyond our control. Furthermore, when we did see each other, as in a Jane Austen novel, we were never alone. Either Ute, her family or friends were present or we were with his family and his friends. We could express ourselves only by hints and gestures which by the nature of things were very open to interpretation. We were both rather enthusiastic writers and in writing letters we would weave carpets of words for each other, beautiful fantasies, sentimental and far away from banal realities. Typically, our understanding improved remarkably when we were not together and only exchanged letters. Whenever we met things quickly became difficult as expectations on both sides were high and were often frustrated.

Our relationship was not made easier by the fact that Ute herself developed a crush on Bernhard while his interest in her was limited. With hindsight it is a miracle that we girls never fell out because of him. Perhaps it was because Bernhard's and my relationship although explicit, mainly lived through our letters, while Ute and Bernhard shared the daily reality at college. My existence always gave them something to talk about. As with many girls with a soft spot for a boy Ute found it awkward to address him directly. However, the fact that she had just received a letter from me always opened Bernhard's door for her. Thus, we both had reason to be envious of each other without being provoked into total despair by seeing the other one utterly happy.

I have to admit that it did not take long before material wishes were mentioned, things he would like; things his family would need urgently. This did cast a shadow across the very idealistic image I had of him, but I quickly brushed any negative feeling aside. I excused his attitude with what the average DDR citizen could know of life in the West. Did not we have similar images about general wealth and abundance in countries like the USA? My financial situation being what it was, of course I could not always fulfil his wishes and I was sorry for this because I do love to give presents.

Very correctly Bernhard soon took me to meet his family. He came from a small village near Weimar. I was made very welcome and quickly became friends with his younger sister with whom I shared preferences for pop groups. We girls were ardent Beatles fans and only argued whether Paul McCarthy (her) or George Harrison (me) was the more attractive, while Bernhard, being male, generally preferred the Rolling Stones.

On one Sunday afternoon I was paraded on a family walk up and down Main Street. Thereafter everybody in the village presumed that this was to indicate that we were finally engaged. If only! Far from being a happy couple, we were closer to a re-enactment of Goethe's 'Sorrows of Young Werther'. This novel was essential reading in both Germanys and even more so in Frankfurt and Weimar. It is the story of a young man who falls in love with a young woman who unfortunately for him is betrothed to another man. After a lot of emotion on all sides, when he realizes that she is happy in her marriage to the other guy, he kills himself. Ever since it was published around 1772 it has been the favourite reading for all world-weary sentimental teenagers with suicidal tendencies.

A year later Bernhard did indeed make a fairly gruesome attempt to take his own life. He went into a wood, took sleeping pills and tried to hang himself from a tree. But the rope broke and he fell to the ground. By that time, he was already unconscious and it was by sheer luck that he was found by passers-by. He remained in hospital for a few weeks and was eventually transferred to a psychiatric unit. From college he was immediately expelled as he had shown himself to be unworthy of teaching future generations of good socialists. To rehabilitate himself he was put into a kitchen to train as a cook. He would have to convince the authorities that after this working experience he was a reformed character to be allowed to return to become a teacher.

Today I am convinced that his world-weariness (or as one would call it in German: *Weltschmerz*) was not primarily caused by our relationship. It was more that a relationship like ours fitted his concept of unavoidable unhappiness perfectly. However, when it happened I felt terribly responsible. I would spend the summer in southern France and from there I wrote to him every day, long letters, although the sun was shining and the sea was most inviting, only to prove the depth of my attachment.

At the end of that year he was on the mend and I could stop worrying so much. But I still wanted to present him with a special gift, something nobody else could give him. Therefore, after I had passed my 'Abitur' in the summer of 1968, I worked very hard to get the money together to be able to invite him to Prague. The then Czechoslovakia was one of the countries East Germans were allowed to visit on a tourist visa. However, it was still something only few people could afford to do and the prospect helped Bernhard to cope with his unsatisfying situation. My savings would pay for the hotel and our expenses. All he had to do was to obtain his visa and to purchase his train ticket.

14. Prague, August 1968

We arrived in Prague on the 18th of August 1968. We smoothed over our awkwardness by talking a lot. It was easy. So much had happened since we had met the last time, so there was a lot to talk about. We pretended to be totally at ease. We did not discuss our relationship. We made no mentioning of the fact that it was the first time we were truly on our own and that the tension between us was palpable. But whatever I might have hoped for, although we kissed and we slept in the same room, nothing more happened. I was much too inexperienced to seduce him and it might have been the same for him. Never mind, we would have plenty of time I thought.

First and foremost, we were busy absorbing the beauties of Prague. I had been there one year before on a school trip. Thus, I could introduce him to the touristy highlights, while he had amassed information about what to do in the evenings and where to party.

It was the years of the 'Prague Spring', a time when the Czechoslovakian government tried to create 'Socialism with a human face' by relaxing the iron grip in which Communist Parties used to hold their people in the countries of the Eastern-bloc. Due to this thaw creativity and experimentations had erupted in all strata of life but especially in the arts. The general mood was far from the dejection that was so typical before and after. While the "Prague Spring" lasted Prague was the perfect place to be.

On the evening of the 20th we saw a wonderful mime show for which Prague was so famous. Afterwards we strolled back to the hotel, singing 'Sympathy for the Devil' by the Rolling Stones, while unbeknown to us Russian tanks were already on the move.

The next morning, we woke up with the feeling that something was wrong. Normally, when we opened the eyes, a radio from the hotel kitchen blared out music into the courtyard our window faced. This morning all we heard were agitated voices talking and shouting. Since I had visited Prague the year before I had studied the Czech language and could communicate on a tourist level but I did not know enough to understand what was being discussed on the radio.

Intrigued we got up, had our breakfast and stepped out of the hotel which was on one of the main streets leading into the city centre. There we saw a tank; and another tank; tank after tank rolling past us. Still we had no idea what was going on. Displays of military strength were regular in communist countries. Therefore, the sight of an army on the move did not frighten us extremely. By the reaction of the onlookers, however, we began to understand that something terrible was happening. One man I spoke to turned around and told us in broken German: "The Russians are here and we don't want them."

Thus, it slowly dawned on us that all the hopes the world had invested in the Prague 'Springtime' were about to be crushed by an invasion of armed forces from different socialist countries headed by the Soviet Union. And our tragic-comic East/West German lovers were stuck in the middle of it.

We began to walk towards Wenceslas Square, the main square, to find out more about what was going on. After about half a mile we came to a corner where the convoy had come to a halt. A great crowd of people seemed to have attacked the army with bare hands, fists and stones. The atmosphere was highly charged. The noise was frightening, the deep roaring of the tank engines, the shouting and crying of the people, a few shots were fired. At least one lorry was in flames. We saw people pushing and shoving in all directions.

Suddenly there was an enormous explosion. The next thing I remember I was crumpled at the foot of a house wall with Bernhard not far from me. Luckily, we were both more or less unscathed. But now shooting had started in earnest. To find shelter we crawled into the next cellar within reach. There we met other people who had hidden here earlier. We were all deeply shocked and anxious about what would happen next. The uprising in the DDR in 1953 and in Hungary in 1956 immediately came to mind and everybody expected nothing less than a bloodbath.

Still we could hear continuous shooting from the street. I knew that I would not sit there waiting like a lamb for the soldiers to come for me. I took Bernhard by the hand and pulled him with me out into the back yard. There was a wall which separated it from the next house's backyard. We climbed this wall and then another into a third backyard, crossed a few houses and back alleys until we eventually ended up at a street which to our surprise was totally quiet and empty. With war raging only a few blocks away it was almost ridiculous how peaceful it felt.

On this lonely empty street, we took time to look at each other. In expectation of a lovely summer day I had sensibly chosen a light blue skirt and a white blouse! These colours had turned into a more fitting refugee's dusty grey. Bernhard did not look his best either. We wound our way through the backstreets of Prague to our hotel, changed into something more adequate for the historical situation and then rushed back to Wenceslas Square.

It took us a day or two to discover that we had ended up in the only bloody battle that had broken out on that day in Prague. The building at the corner whose windows were smashed already by bullets when we first arrived was the main radio station. The invaders had order to shut down all means of public communications to prevent any developing resistance from spreading information. This was exactly why spontaneously Czechs had tried to defend the building. Four people had died there. The lorry, which had caught fire, unfortunately had been loaded with ammunition. The driver and those sitting on the lorry fled without warning the people around.

Eventually the ammunition on the lorry exploded which caused all that damage.

Despite all this I was not really frightened or in a panic. Except for those few moments when I must have lost consciousness immediately after the explosion, I always knew what I was doing and what I wanted to do. I wanted to survive and get out of it! On those few occasions in my life, when I found myself in severe danger, I am glad to say I always reacted very coolly and never lost my head in any sense of the word.

It was twenty years later in the darkness of a cinema that very belatedly I suddenly suffered the panic I was spared then. We saw Milan Kundera's 'The Unbearable Lightness of Being'. In that movie they had included the original footage of the battle around the radio station. I did not recognize us but I did recognize the moment and suddenly I started to tremble in an overwhelming panic and it took me quite a while to find my way back into the reality of the cinema.

During the first hours of that historic day wherever we went and to whomever we spoke utter sadness and grief was the prevalent emotion. One man told us, crying: "We are a people of Quislings (infamous collaborator during the Nazi-occupation of Norway) and we will do it again this time!" Rumours went around: the government was already arrested, deported to Moscow and shot there on arrival. Only the first two parts turned out to be correct. Names of probable traitors circulated, politicians who might have conspired with the Soviets and other secret services planning to terminate the historic experiment. It later turned out that there were some grains of truth in what was spread. Like everybody we absorbed every bit of information eagerly.

However, after the first twenty-four hours we and the rest of the world realised with awe that this time things would be very, very different. Something happened which had never happened before. A very witty and sophisticated form of peaceful resistance developed which aroused a feeling of proud and absolute euphoria in everybody who took part in it.

One of the most impressive features of those days was the way people found a way to organise themselves. There was hardly any state authority any more, as the Czech Police and Army had been neutralised. Their highest level of command was arrested and replaced by Soviet officers. Subsequently soldiers and policemen simply refused to obey orders. But what had to been done still worked like clockwork and nobody exploited the situation for their own advantage.

On each square downtown Russian tanks were stationed, their heavy guns swinging around menacingly, soldiers sitting on top with their guns ready to shoot. But no attempt was made to attack them with guns or rifles. Thus, their weapons were good for nothing. They were attacked by being talked to incessantly. This was the last thing these soldiers were prepared for. Very civil people obviously totally harmless and unarmed gathered around the tanks and asked the individual soldier intelligent questions like "Why are you here?", "What do you know about us?" "What have they told you?", "Do you realise that you had been lied to?"

With my own eyes I saw soldiers weeping after they had been asked for the thousandth time: "Where is the counter revolution you are supposed to fight?" "Whom are you fighting? Do you see a single weapon raised against you?"

I was quite close, when one soldier in despair suddenly lifted his gun and began to shoot just to shut up his interrogators. Everybody ducked and took cover until his comrades quickly managed to stop him. Fortunately, nobody was hit, but it was a very tense moment.

There were even some comical moments. Since the Second World War there had never been foreign troops stationed in Czechoslovakia, thus the occupiers had no base. And as the preparation for the invasion was done in absolute secrecy they could not prepare any infrastructure for themselves. They had only what they had on their tanks and their lorries.

Of course, after sitting around on their tanks for hours in the middle of town the soldiers had very urgent human needs. However, they had been ordered not to provoke the population. Neither were they allowed to break into houses nor to perform in public what they urgently needed to do. Thus, they were reduced to going around, knocking at doors and politely asking if they could please use the toilet, which generally was forcefully denied. Simultaneously –

surprise, surprise - all the public lavatories were suddenly rendered unusable. Eventually in desperation soldiers with rifles levelled fought their way to one public toilet building which had not yet been destroyed. They broke the doors open and from then on, an endless queue of soldiers in need waiting their turn could be observed there day and night.

Under the eyes of the frustrated military, creative resistance went on. Activities ran like a river around the islands on which the occupiers sat. While avoiding direct confrontation it streamed along wherever it was possible. The occupiers just did not know how to handle this obviously unarmed mass of people who gathered and then dispersed as quickly as they came together.

There was one square where people continuously painted anti-occupation posters and hung them to dry on clothes lines from which other people took them away to different parts of the city and mount them there. One very popular slogan was: "Lenin, please rise! Brezhnev has just gone crazy!" When soldiers interfered on the square, the artists just moved aside and took their open-air workshop to another corner.

The illegal radio stations which had sprung up quickly gave advice or orders like: "No alcohol!" and all pubs immediately ceased selling alcohol so that no one under the influence of alcohol could in his desperation have endangered his own or other peoples' lives. And if you know how much Czechs love their beer you have to admit that this was a show of remarkable discipline.

Another essential order via radio was: "Destroy all street-signs! The Russians don't have reliable maps." Within an hour there was no street sign left in all of Prague and the rest of the country. It was easy: each individual had only to remove the one sign he had in front of him. With millions of people all ready to do their bid it worked like clockwork. At every street corner you could see two or three people on steps or on car roofs patiently working away with their screwdrivers until the sign in question came down.

The invasion must have been prepared in such haste, that the Russians indeed did depend on ordinary city maps. So, with the street names and any kind of directions vanished they were quite helpless. I have heard, but it might not be true, that one official radio station continued on air for a few days longer simply by exchanging their front door plaque for one of a near-by kindergarten.

Rumour had been partly correct about those top members of the party and the government, who had supported the Prague Spring. They had indeed been arrested and taken to an unknown place, which later turned out to be Moscow. But soon it leaked out where they were and that they were still alive. So, to save them was one of the aims of the general resistance and probably the biggest success of all was that not a single person was executed and that they were returned to Prague within a few days.

Word went around that more arrests were

planned. The number plates of the cars driven by those supposedly carrying out those arrests were published over the illegal radio stations. Within a few hours the same stations were proudly telling their listeners that all such cars were now beyond use as ordinary car drivers had sacrificed their cars and risked their lives and health by using their own cars as tools to render the secret service cars unusable.

The contribution of the illegal radio stations proved to be so decisive that within days the occupiers started to broadcast themselves, pretending it was another illegal station, to confuse the public. However, their transmissions could easily be identified by their slogans – the main message being how as good comrades the occupiers had bravely saved the country from a counterrevolutionary clique - and also by the way in which they mispronounced certain words.

Faced with a moment of history our little private drama lost all its importance. Already on the first day we became involved with the resistance against the occupiers and ended up working for one of the many illegal radio stations. My Czech was still poorly but it was good enough to translate their bad German into a correct version. The texts we produced collectively then were transmitted into the DDR and to the DDR troops on Czech soil.

During the hours of daylight, we felt quite safe. We served our part from a private flat, sitting together like a group of friends. The transmitter was in another building, with a guard watching it from the house opposite. A messenger went there now and again, fed the tapes into the machine and left as quickly as possible, which was the really dangerous part. If the Russians should be able to detect anything, it would be the transmitter, which would give us time to get away. So, it felt a bit like a teach-in with people coming and going, smoking lots of cigarettes (Sorry! Those were the times) and drinking lots of very black coffee.

It was very different at night. There was a curfew and the only movement on the street came from the occupying forces. On the first night we stayed with our new friends. Unfortunately, during this night my father managed to phone our hotel. This was sensational because the few telephone lines which existed were either cut or totally overloaded. But he had been successful only to learn that the hotel had no idea of my whereabouts. He nearly had a heart attack. Like anyone else he had followed the news eagerly and had of course heard about the curfew.

Therefore, every night I tried to get back to the hotel - curfew or not - in case the telephone should work again for a few hours. That meant running from our friends back to the hotel, through empty dark streets, hiding behind whatever was there when we heard the recognisable sound of a military vehicle approaching. On one occasion we had reached the locked and bolted door of the hotel and knocked when suddenly we had to hide once more. The hotel door opened, somebody looked out but of course he could not see us hidden behind the litterbins. So, he closed and locked the door again. We rushed back to the door and knocked again. But another vehicle approached and we had to throw ourselves again behind our litterbins. Only at the third attempt were we eventually able to reach the safety of the hotel lounge.

Our visas had long expired, but who cared! We just stayed on and the hotel did not mind as expected guests would hardly arrive under those circumstances. Service in the hotel was replaced by a rather spontaneous muddling through by all and everybody. We ate and drank what came to hand. The whole country was in a kind of general strike; thus, shops were visibly emptying and deliveries to the hotel ceased.

We lived from day to day in an emotional state of emergency mixed with phases of absolute elation. My feeling at the time was - and still remains today - that it was a tragedy that the invasion happened. But as it had to happen, I was glad I was there. I have hardly ever felt so utterly alive and in the handful of situations, when the going got really tough, I realised that I loved life and that I desired to survive at all costs. I realised that as far as I had ever joined in with Bernhard's world-weariness, it was nothing but the fashionable and superficial attitude of a stupid teenager.

I have no idea what Bernhard's real feelings were during those days. Other than me he was under considerable pressure. He had to explain and excuse himself again and again because he came from one of the countries which were involved in the occupation. Czechs then distinguished very strictly between East and West Germans, with those from the east being despised and those from the west being treated as best friends. On one occasion Bernhard listened to me while I explained that I came from West Germany and only nodded as if I had answered for the two of us. "Did I really do this? Denying where I come from?" he asked desperately when we were alone again. But I could really understand him. Emotions understandably ran raw and more than often he was personally insulted.

Of course, Bernhard never tried to justify what was happening. Nobody we met did at that time. He was absolutely against the invasion, I am sure of that. We even discussed whether it could be an opportunity for him to come with me to West Germany. Naively we calculated that under those circumstances the Czech border police might look the other way and allow us both through.

But in the end Bernhard took the decision to return to the DDR. In a way he was a bit passive and most certainly he was a romantic. Perhaps the perspective to live in a foreign country frightened him. He would have had little opportunity to ever seeing his family and friends again, and even worse he would depend on someone who had turned out to be not so much a damsel in distress but a rebellious daredevil.

After about two weeks or more some uniformed

men came to the hotel. I don't know whether they were police, secret service or military personnel. They told us unmistakably to get lost. We promised to leave as soon as possible. The next morning, they came back to make sure we were on our way. They accompanied us to different railway stations where trains waited to take unwanted foreigners to the borders. They allowed us a few moments to say our farewells and that was the last I ever saw of Bernhard.

Unfortunately, at home he got into trouble again because of his Prague adventures. He was arrested and questioned about his activities in Prague. He insisted he was nothing more than a tourist who had got caught up in the invasion. Eventually they had to release him because they could not prove any kind of counterrevolutionary actions. I was not surprised that by then he was totally disenchanted with me and all the upheaval I had brought into his life. Not long after our encounter with world history I heard that he had gotten married and that was the end of our bitter sweet love story.

After the 'Wende' in 1989 Bernhard actually contacted me again but I thought I would rather keep my memories deep in my emotional drawer, wrapped with a faded pink ribbon, and so I wrote him a letter declining to re-establishing any contacts or to meet him again.

15. Are we grown-ups now or what?

Although one of my East-West relationships had come to a sad end neither world history nor any man could come between Ute and me. Some people say that blood is thicker than water, and for us that is certainly true. Like siblings we can't really get rid of each other.

However, it took three years or more before we saw each other again. We then must have been twenty-two-ish. I had passed my first exam in sociology and had moved from Frankfurt to Munich to continue my studies there. I was poorer than ever. I had to earn every Deutsche Mark I spent. My parents were no longer in the position to support me as my father had lost his job and for a while he was unemployed. Due to some strange rule which related a scholarship to the parental income of two years previously when my father's income was still above the limit, I could not get any support when I needed it most.

Munich was and still is an expensive place. Lots of needy students were competing for cheap accommodation and temporary jobs. Although I worked very hard I had to live very frugal and travelling to Erfurt had become a luxury because the DDR asked every visitor to change 10, - DM per day. The exchange rate was 1:1, although a realistic rate probably would have been 1:15. For the DDR it was a welcome source for hard currency and a method to keep visitors away. For me it meant that I only could afford this entrance fee for a few days now and then.

In Erfurt much had happened in-between. Ute's beloved grandfather Hermann had passed away and only six months later she also lost her father. He had been ailing for a very long time and yet the end came very suddenly. He died only a few days before Ute had been due to take her final exam. Although the exam board offered to postpone her exam to a later date, she insisted on carrying on as planned. Of course, she passed, although afterwards she told me she could remember nothing of what went on as she felt so numb.

And then there were her wedding plans. Knowing about the fragility of her father, Eberhard, her husband-to-be, and she had set the date with so much hope that her father would still be amongst them but it was not to be. Still they went ahead with the wedding as her father would have wished it and as her mother encouraged her to do. However, it was a quiet and rather solemn affair.

They tied the knot out of love but to get married had also practical advantages. It was an achievement that her grandfather had held onto his house, while many house owners had given in to pressure and handed over theirs to the state. By marrying and starting a family Ute was able to keep onto the house, which otherwise would have been declared too big for her and her mother. Either they would have had to accept the house being split up into flats or they even might have been forced to hand it over to the authorities which allocated accommodations according to family sizes. During the forty years the DDR existed there was always a shortage of housing. As rents were kept artificially low, the market had to be controlled. For accommodation one had to apply and give good reasons for doing so, one of them being marriage and children. Then one had to wait until the top of the list was reached and then there was not much choice. One had to take what was allocated.

Considering all the usual shortages the DDR took an enormous effort to build as many houses as fast as possible. Today we look with horror at the uniformity of block after block of houses which were constructed all over the country in the same manner. They were so stereotyped that people could explain what their flat looked like by simply mentioning the flat type. However, for many people it was the first time they ever had central heating, a proper indoor toilet and a bathroom with hot and cold taps, not to mention the fitted kitchen. It was a worthwhile reason to tie the knot as fast as possible.

But the urge to get married was not only due to these circumstances. The general attitude even amongst young people in the DDR was that if a female was not married and with child by the age of twenty, something was wrong with her, and I know that Ute 'already' being twenty-two was a bit anxious at being considered a wallflower because she took her time to choose wisely.

East Germans married much earlier than West

Germans. There starting a family and having as many children as possible was supported by the state with a lot of privileges. Due to the mass exodus before the Wall and the persistent low productivity the country urgently needed growth in the work force, so everything was done to encourage people to become parents. But there was ambivalence due to the fact that women too were urgently needed in the workforce and pregnancies could be disruptive. Therefore, as much as having children was encouraged, abortions were legal and frequent. The other side of the coin was that as quickly as people got married, they then filed for divorce. This was easy to obtain. In a broader sense, marrying and divorcing replaced what in a more permissive society might be called "gathering experiences".

Moral rules remained more strictly adhered to in the DDR than I was accustomed within my sphere. I came from a liberal family, and Frankfurt, where I grew up, was one of the West German centres of the youth revolt that went around the world in the late sixties, which among other demands included the perspective of a more liberated sexuality. To me it seemed that the general mood in the DDR in comparison was still one of inhibition. Likewise, these strict codes of behaviour were often hypocritical as one would expect in a society which kept it members under permanent observation.

An excessive degree of neighbourly or workplace related control was part of the political program. In all aspects of everyday life, in schools, at work and in the neighbourhood, people were organised in 'collectives'. These collectives had to take responsibility for their common achievements or lack of them. For instance, if one member of the collective turned out to have problems with alcohol, it was the collective that was supposed to do something about it and was disciplined for not succeeding. Collective responsibility provided strong incentives to keep each other on the straight and narrow, and whoever stepped out of line was considered suspicious. There was little freedom even in the most personal relationships and hardly any space for experiments.

While I spent my time moving from one relationship into another, falling in love, falling out of love, trying out what living together with a man could mean, leaving or being abandoned by the gentleman in question, shedding a lot of tears or even smiling, I was always sure that I would never get married. I felt I still had plenty of opportunities to decide on what I wanted to do with my life while for Ute her adult life had already begun. When I arrived in Erfurt the next time not only was she a fully qualified teacher, she was already a wife and a mother. From the start she was determined to make her marriage work, and she and Eberhard succeeded. They are still married and today are years past their silver wedding anniversary.

The old house had been remodelled again. Her mother Gerti restricted herself to the ground floor, where the kitchen was, and the young family lived on the first floor. Ute tells me that they even had a lodger then but I can't remember a fourth person in the house. The only bathroom on the first floor was to be shared by everybody. But there was no kitchen in Ute's realm. Therefore, they had converted the smallest room into a place to cook. Eberhard had done his best to make it work, but the general shortage of building material meant that there were no water taps and no sink and Ute had to carry every drop of water to and from the bathroom for many years.

Their baby daughter, Susanne, was a lovely and healthy baby. Bright and strong, she was called: "the lioness". Ute now faced the education system not only as a teacher but also as a parent. The intention of the DDR system of child-welfare was that the state had the first right and duty to bring up and educate children. This superseded even the parents' rights. Crèches were on offer for babies from the age of a few months, followed by kindergarten. Afterwards while traditionally school in both Germanys was restricted to the morning hours, every school had programs to supervise children in the afternoon. All these institutions opened very early in the morning, around 7 am, to make sure that parents would be at their work place right on time. This allowed women to return to their jobs as quickly as possible after giving birth. Whether this was done to support women's emancipation is open to debate. While the number of women in jobs was much higher in the East than it was in the West, there was hardly any discussion about what else women's emancipation could mean. Relations within families - as far as I witnessed them - were very traditional in their division of responsibilities. Men were always seen as the main breadwinners and the heads of the family, while women's work included most of the housework and the care of the children. Arguably there were more women in higher ranks of politics and professions than in the West but numbers were still far from parity.

What always made me suspicious about how women understood their own position in the East was the fact that they did not even consider that there could be any problems. I for one had a problem with their job titles. In their professional life women were addressed like men although the German language allows male and female titles in the majority of cases by simply adding an ~in to the male title (male teacher = Lehrer, female teacher = Lehrerin, male carpenter = Tischler, female carpenter = Tischlerin). Whenever I mentioned this idiosyncrasy I was told that this was not significant and that to be addressed as an "honorary" man just showed how proud women were of their profession. Still today I wonder why things should have to be male to give women the right to be proud.

The explicit intention of all educational efforts was to develop – that phrase again - the 'rounded socialist personality'. Consequently, the groups of children under supervision were quite large. Individuality was not encouraged and fitting into the group was the overriding concern. Even potty training followed a dogma: all children were collectively placed on pots at certain times and only then. Although as a teacher Ute was part of the socialist education system, as a parent she felt she did not want her child to be taken over by the state at too early a stage and so Susanne skipped crèche.

However, Ute was eager to return to her professional life when her daughter was ready to go to kindergarten. At this time there was a shortage of kindergarten places in their area and so, to Ute's frustration, she had to wait for a while. We had lengthy discussions about this delay and I explained that in West Germany, where there were always shortages of suitable and affordable kindergarten places, people had started to organise childcare themselves. This movement was called: "Kinderladen (children's shop)" as many of these self-organised groups rented premises that were sufficiently spacious and inexpensive as they had stood empty with the rise of supermarkets and the decline of corner shops. An important aim of this movement was of course to bring up children in a less authoritarian atmosphere than that of the average state-run or church-run kindergarten. However, the practical aspect of having the children in their own vicinity without paying over the top, and having a say in choosing the staff, were equally important to the parents.

Hence, I proposed that Ute could try to find other mothers in her area who were waiting for kindergarten places and to organise a private childminding group. Ute, however, made it clear very quickly that there was no way she could do this. Any formation of an association for whatever reason, which was not officially sanctioned, would not be tolerated. It would be for a worthwhile reason, I tried to argue. Most certainly they should be allowed to proceed, as it would help to relieve the shortage of kindergarten places. On the contrary, Ute said, it would be close to treason. Officially there were no shortages in the social system. And things which *could* not happen in socialism *did* not happen! As there was no shortage, there was no reason to do something about it. Also, if she criticised the shortage of kindergarten places in any way, she was simply spreading the propaganda of the enemy and thus would be considered to be a foreign agent.

There were other examples and I started to understand that this mechanism worked everywhere. Soon I was convinced that such a system of dealing with reality was mad and doomed. One of Ute's friends from student days, who already worked as a teacher while Ute was still caring for Susanne, provided me with another valid example. At the end of each school year every teacher had to write a report about which goals had been achieved. In education, as in any other sphere of life it was essential to fulfil a plan and if possible to exceed the demanded targets. This young teacher, when he had handed in his first annual report, had listed all facts truthfully and identified where he had been successful in fulfilling the plan and where he had not. He was utterly surprised when he was summoned in front of a committee and faced not only hostile questioning but a lot of pressuring to change his report for the better. Older colleagues beseeched him not to be stupid. None of them ever admitted failure. They recorded what was expected and not a sentence more.

The historical tragedy lay in the fact that those individual reports were assembled into a school report which showed that every plan was exceeded. Then it went from town to district to central government, each level embellishing the statements again and again until the highest level could proudly declare that their school system was near to perfection. The thus fulfilled or more-than-fulfilled plan would then be revised for the following period with even higher targets. Thus, plan and reality grew farther and farther apart. If I remember correctly this friend of Ute's sustained his attitude for three years before he eventually gave in and followed the example of his colleagues, tired of being bullied again and again.

Of course, the main problem for a society where everything is planned centrally is: how does one define success and how can one measure it? An open market where products could prove their value by being sold at their market-prices did not exist. Market-prices consist of costs of production, costs of administration and the expected profit which depends on competition and customer demand. When prices are made according to political aims, the amount you sell tells you nothing. So, they had to invent other measuring devices. If I remember correctly there was a time when in the metal processing industry success was measured by the amount of steel which was used. Can you imagine the size of the sewing needles this industry produced if judged only by in-put? You could not make a proper stitch with those needles, but at least they used a lot of steel, didn't they?

The same mechanism worked in every sector whether it was production or social coherence. Wherever success was demanded it was claimed rightly or wrongly. Those on top who had to decide about new plans and plan-fulfilment could never have had an idea of what was really happening. No wonder they were never able to manage their plans to the satisfaction of the needs of their population.

In schools this system of embellishing the truth handed over some power to the pupils. They learnt quickly enough that their teachers would be judged by their, the pupil's success. Therefore, more than once an unspoken understanding would evolve between teachers and pupils in the sense that the latter would get better marks for average results if they only kept up the appearance of discipline.

Ute told me that this was especially the case for those students who, while still in school, already had signed up to join the army as professional soldiers. East and West Germany had conscription armies, where recruits served for a limited time. Those who aimed for a career as an officer came from the much more limited number of volunteers. However, to progress through the ranks was restricted to those with outstanding school results and so the school would be informed and advised not to stand in the way of these promising young men. In plain speaking this meant that their marks were expected go up remarkably and immediately. It was rumoured that some young men even used this unwritten rule to leave school with top marks only to change their minds afterwards. Instead of joining the army they rather applied for a place at university which was happily granted to them due to their excellent school results.

Eventually even I felt the consequences of that attitude. At the time of the 'Wende' 1989 I managed vocational training courses of adults. In one of our computer courses the majority of participants happened to come from the former DDR. These courses were funded by the job centre to enable people to re-enter the job-market.

Shortly after the course had started it was obvious that there were a lot of problems. I had to visit the students on more than one occasion to tell them that if they did not work harder they would not pass the final tests. They looked at me with utter surprise and their "speaker" suggested in all earnestness that I would not dare to fail them all as this would rebound on me and the institution I represented. Then she grinned and leaned back satisfied that she had beaten me with one stroke while the rest nodded their heads in agreement.

I replied that I had a surprise for them. The high

standard of our teaching and our tests were more important to me than their individual fate. How better to prove our standards than with a result where 80% had failed? At the end of the day it would be them who would have to face the consequences. Without having passed the test the labour-exchange would stop paying for their maintenance and would thank me for proving that they were not worthy of public support. And I could not refrain from adding that they still had to learn a lot and not only how to handle a computer. In the end still more than 50 % of this group failed and found out that my predictions were absolutely correct.

By the way, this was the last time I ever heard the famous sentence that "the collective had taken the decision that..." Whenever massive conflicts happened in one of our courses I had made it a rule to allow each individual to speak in turn and uninterrupted to inform the group, their lecturer and myself about what they thought of the course and its conditions. In the majority of cases this calmed down heated arguments and successfully reminded our participants that in the end they were adults and had to shoulder a certain responsibility for their words and actions.

When I suggested it on this occasion the "speaker" suddenly got very excited and proclaimed that the collective had already taken a decision and that she spoke for the rest. As she elaborated on her position in this 'collective' I developed a strong feeling that the majority of the group were intimidated by her and therefore remained silent. Needless to say, that when I told her that I was still very interested in hearing what each individual thought, and, with her permission, we would now proceed as I had suggested, the reaction and the result was very different from what she had offered as the will of the majority.

But let us return to developments in the DDR in the sixties and seventies. The general attitude about maintaining the fiction that everything in the country and with the system was perfect had more sinister aspects. On one occasion I visited my cousin Karl-Heinz in Dresden. Together we went to see his wife's family who lived in a village nearby. When we arrived, everybody was in a state of shock because his sister-in-law had been raped a few days before. It had happened on a path through woods which connected the bus station to the village. As if the fact in itself was not horrible enough, when the victim went to the police to report the crime she learnt that she was the third female to have been raped on this pathway within a few months. In every case the culprit had escaped unrecognised and thus was still at large.

Infuriated the young woman demanded to know why nobody had warned the women of the village. A very depressed police officer informed her that the DDR was a peaceful and progressive country and so crime was unknown, unlike in the West which was rife with it. Therefore, unfortunately they were not entitled to inform people about criminal behaviour even if it occasionally occurred. Public knowledge would only assist the enemy's schemes against the DDR. However, if she as a private person would not mind going around warning the women in the village they would overlook the fact that she would be spreading hostile propaganda.

Ute was not at all surprised when I told her this story. The antagonism between her own perceptions and the official version of the facts was something she tried to live with as did everybody else. It was not easy. The human psyche seems to protest against being forced to believe the unbelievable. At one time Ute became so desperate that she consulted a psychiatrist. Only then did she learn how many people actually had similar troubles. It was not that psychological problems were accepted as such, and psychotherapy or psychoanalysis was denounced as bourgeois, but the psychosomatic results of the permanent stress took their toll and many people were taking medication of one kind or another in order to cope with this state decreed schizophrenia.

16. The sixties and their politics

Now, there also was a lot of thought-control where I came from – it was just a bit subtler. It was not that you would feel under permanent surveillance. We lived in a state founded on the rule of law, where you could think and say what you wanted. There were people who went to prison because they belonged to the forbidden Communist Party, but nobody forced you to agree to everything the ruling party declared.

We were free to make up our own minds but there were a lot of taboos, things you just did not express even if you thought them, and most of the time you did not even allow your thoughts to go along that line. You might have ideas, but if you didn't have a framework in which to express yourself, because words like capitalism and socialism were strictly taboo, you would find it difficult to communicate your convictions. On the other hand, if the generally accepted expressions were repeated again and again, you would use them without further reflection and by using them you would become part of a system that avoided certain truths.

For instance: what you called the DDR gave an indication of where you stood politically. You could address the state next door as 'Zone', 'Ostzone (Eastern zone)' 'SBZ (Sowjetisch besetzte Zone=soviet occupied zone)', 'sogenannte (so called) DDR' or 'DDR'. If you put words down in writing you had to put DDR in inverted commas (like "DDR") to indicate that you understood this construct did not really exist. The state, the government, their institutions, everything was 'so called'. To forget it or to leave it out on purpose was valid proof that you were an open or a cryptic communist. 'Red' or 'communist' were strong insults.

Into this attitude was mixed a general hatred of 'Russians', who were portrayed as dangerous or in the tradition of the Nazis with strong racial undertones as sub-human dirty slit-eyed rapists. These images were used to vilify everybody considered to be 'left'. In an early general election, the Christian Democrats in their advertisements associated the picture of a bloodthirsty Russian with the Social Democratic Party. It was successful not only in winning the vote but also in creating general agreement about what was evil.

I was fourteen when I joined the German branch of the CND. At Easter 1964 we were not more than 3000 people who marched for three days through more or less unpopulated countryside and through empty backwaters of Frankfurt as we were not allowed on the main streets. To use loudspeakers was forbidden, but cunningly the organisers had placed a jazz band on the back of a lorry and they made enough noise to bring people to their windows and balconies. The good burgesses of Frankfurt shook their heads and turned away in disgust, while the Young Conservatives hunted us through the streets to beat us up.

Two years later, in 1966, nobody could stop us anymore from taking to the main streets. Tens of thousands were on the street and we had impressive floats. People like Joan Baez and Wolfgang Biermann performed at the final rally on the main square in Frankfurt. Eventually at the peak in 1968 there were more than 30,000 participants in Frankfurt alone and that was only one of many marches in West Germany.

However, in 1964 when I wore a small CND button in school (we do not have school uniforms in Germany) it caused uproar amongst teachers and had it not been for my classmates I might even have been expelled. One day after word had gone around that I was threatened with expulsion, half of my form wore the very same button and that was the end of any threats.

It was our generation which began to rebel against the rigidity of the political and social system. It was the end of deference towards the authorities whether they were parents, teachers or government. In Germany, where historically obedience was something of a national epidemic, it was unheard of and in the beginning the authorities were stunned. In protest against what we were taught to accept as eternal truth we began to study Marx, Freud and everyone else who offered us alternative explanations from the ones we had been force-fed throughout the fifties and early sixties.

Society's reaction wavered between uncertain sympathy and harsh repulsion. At Frankfurt University there was a time when even professors addressed their audience as "comrades". I remember one lecturer handing out copies of a valuable magazine which he wanted returned afterwards and while doing so he made this unforgettable statement: "Comrades! I hope we all agree that pinching would be counter-revolutionary, don't we?" His name was Christian von Krokow and people then addressed him as "Comrade Earl Krokow".

However, these were a few progressive and probably quite sheltered islands within a sea of utter consternation of those whose framework of ideas had not changed much since the Third Reich. More than once while taking part in some political activity I heard that 'we should all be sent to labour camps' or even 'to the gas chamber' and that 'things like that would never have happened under Hitler'.

To make the majority of the older generation understand what we were all about was not easy. My generation was upset about the injustice and repression we witnessed around us. We had discovered the past of our fathers and grandfathers and we protested against old Nazis working as teachers or in any position of influence. For us the break with the past had not been radical enough. We demanded to have a say in what we were taught in schools and universities. We demanded more rights for the working classes.

After many years of conservative (CDU/CSU) governments we were now (since 1966) governed by a grand coalition of the main parties CDU and SPD.

This left the small liberal party (FDP) as the only opposition. In numbers: of 518 MPs 468 supported the government. This was not our idea of democracy. So, we took the opposition to the street and very quickly the name APO (Außerparlamentarische Opposition) stuck.

Worldwide there were lots of causes to drive us to the barricades. We rallied against the Shah of Persia and the Vietnam War. The tabloid press in Germany demonised us. We organised boycotts against them. There were first martyrs, Benno Ohnesorg, shot and killed 1967 by an over-excited policeman and of course Rudi Dutschke, who was shot by a fanaticised reader of the same tabloid press and died later as a consequence of his injuries.

This assassination attempt in spring 1968 was the spark which triggered the Federal Republic to explode. I still remember the font cover of one of the most popular weekly journal "Der Stern" of the following week. On a fuzzy image of demonstrators being hit by a water canon were placed these words: "Is the revolution still stoppable?" It was a serious question and everyone including ourselves had the feeling that it needed just one more forceful push for the system to tumble.

It was an illusion. The government proposed bringing in a law permitting for dictatorial powers in vaguely defined national emergencies. We felt that this law was directed against any form of opposition. If you looked back at the way the Nazis had come to power in the thirties, this fear was justified and not just paranoia. A gigantic nation-wide anti-campaign ensued, but failed in the end. The general strike we so very much hoped for did not materialise and the law went through backed by the above mentioned overwhelming parliamentary majority.

The following period often was called 'The Leaden Time'. The establishment, which had been stunned previously, now hit back in any way possible while resistance crumbled. A mass movement founded on a handful of fundamental ideas shared by all ended up totally fragmented. For those who were alienated from politics altogether, there was sex, drugs and rock'n'roll, flower-power and peace, religious sects and psychotherapies and sometimes a wild mixture of all of these. On the radical left a hundred and one different factions formed which fought more amongst themselves than against capitalism, the establishment or the authorities. There were some who started 'the long march through the institutions' trying to bring change to the system from within. They joined political parties and trade unions. They finished their education and set off on their careers. The Schröder-(SPD/Greens, 1998 - 2005) government consisted mostly of those who had successfully completed this "long march". It makes one feel a bit nostalgic to look at old pictures of those long haired, wild lefties who today wear their bespoke suits with pride. And unfortunately, there were a handful who turned to terrorism (RAF= Rote Armee Faction) and thus provided the state with an excuse for a general witch hunt.

The hopes of those who still held some trust in traditional politics were rekindled enormously when in 1969 Willy Brandt became the first social democratic chancellor of the Federal Republic and survived a vote of no-confidence in 1972.

The new government a coalition of Social Democrats and Liberals (FDP) made a profound change in policy towards the communist countries. In 1970 Brandt himself even went to Erfurt (!) to meet there with Willy Stoph, the then Prime Minister of the DDR. This was a revolutionary act because as the West German government had always denied that the DDR existed at all there could consequently be no government to which one could talk.

During the visit in 1970 thousands gathered in front of the hotel where the meeting took place and shouted "Willy, Willy", until eventually Willy Stoph came to the window. Then the masses changed their chant to "Willy Brandt, Willy Brandt" to make it clear whom they really wished to see and to cheer.

Although I agreed with the foreign policy of the new government, not all was well with domestic affairs. Brandt had entered his office promising "to dare more democracy". However, one of the first decrees the new administration published was one against 'radicals' (Radikalenerlass). It made it impossible to enter public services if one was suspected of not standing 'firmly on the liberal democratic basic order' (auf den Grundlagen der freiheitlich demokratisch Grundordnung stehen – only in German can you construct such a monster of a sentence). We shortened it quickly to FDGO and suffered the consequences because it meant that whoever was under suspicion of being a "radical" could not become a teacher or a policeman, could not deliver mail, drive a train or take any other employment in the public services.

On one of my returns from the DDR I learnt that a file with my name on it existed in West Germany. This was in 1973. I had spent a few days in Erfurt while the World Youth Festival took place in that part of Berlin which then was the capital of the DDR. On that occasion it was the West German border control that went through the train with long lists of names.

When they came across my name, they suddenly confronted me with the charge that I must have been at the festival. I denied it. They insisted and told me that if I should admit to having been there they would allow me to travel on. Otherwise they had to arrest me. I remained stubborn and they guided me from the train into a building where they questioned me for two hours.

The interrogation was a bit kafkaesque. They asked me again and again to prove that I had not been taking part in the festival. I tried to explain that philosophically it would be quite difficult to prove something non-existing. Was it not up to them to prove that I *was* there? They were not amused, suspected I was taking the mickey. Eventually I found some tram tickets I still had in my pocket as proof that at least at some time during the period in question I had been in Erfurt. This was all I could provide them with, so they let me go and allowed me to board the next train. It was obvious that my name was registered and as long as this decree (Radikalenerlass) was enforced I never even tried to apply for a job in the public services.

Of course, the pressure I might have been under was nothing compared with Ute's situation. In West Germany all you had to have was a bit of civil courage plus limited ambitions, and you could live your life more or less as you wanted. In many areas neither the state nor society would interfere too much. Indeed, I had my fair share of the sex, drugs and rock'n'roll that was on offer. I could meet freely with my friends; we could form political groups and new initiatives. We could join demonstrations and from time to time get into trouble with the police. Nobody forced us into the general double-think-system Ute and her friends had to practice.

In all socialist states there existed two realities side by side, still one excluding the other. One was a reflection of all the experiences the individual made which were only shared in the privacy of the most intimate relationships. The other was an official *TRUTH*, which had to be declared publicly again and again in a permanent gesture of submissiveness. People had both in their heads, switched between them depending on the circumstances, sometimes balancing the act cynically and sometimes going mad because of it.

Again, I came upon this phenomenon later when I organised courses for Russian-Germans who migrated to Germany in tens of thousands from Siberia once it was allowed. In those courses we tried to explain to them how our society and our social system worked. How health, unemployment and old age were financially subsidised by compulsory insurance; what kind of schools were there for their children; what they had to do to receive benefits; how to rent a flat and all the other necessities of life in a new and unknown culture.

On more than one occasion the information which they traded among themselves contradicted profoundly with those we had presented and we hardly ever managed to convince them that ours was correct and that theirs was nonsense. What really unnerved many of our teachers was that they never argued. The nodded agreeably and then they went and did the opposite. In their eyes we were nothing but the representatives of the system. We were powerful therefore they were eager to make every gesture of submission. But they did not believe a word of what we said because we just had to be lying as every authority had always lied to them. Their own network was the only reliable source for them and nothing would change that presumption.

17. A Day in School

Had in 1975 a fairy allowed us a glimpse into the beginning of the next century, we would not have believed it. In 1975 the two great blocs headed by the USA and the USSR respectively seemed set in stone for all eternity. All we could do was to accept it and to deal with the fact that two German states existed. All we could hope for was that with decreasing tension, relations between the two German states would normalise to the point that citizens of both sides could keep in contact and eventually travel freely. And there was the prospect that in 2011 Ute would retire from work and would then be able to visit me in West Germany.

I never supported those who thought that we should starve the East into submission. It had been tried and it had only made things worse. I never believed that peace would be safer by amassing more and more weapons. The capacity for a threefold overkill compared with a twofold, with both Germanys as the main battleground, did nothing to make me feel more secure.

Like many I hoped that if the existence of the DDR would be accepted worldwide, their government would probably feel more secure and would ease the many restrictions with which their citizens had to cope. I expressed these ideas on one occasion when Ute took me to an 'International Women's day (8th of March)' reception given by her school for all female teachers. I ended up at a table with her headmaster and we had a very animated discussion around the table about many aspects of this very complex question. At the end of the afternoon the headmaster expressed himself quite enthusiastic about the discussion and asked me whether I would like to come to his school and have a discussion with his pupils.

And so, one morning I accompanied Ute to her school. There in turn I faced four classes of students in their final year for one lesson each. A teacher was always present and most of the time the headmaster himself was in the room as well. However, in no way did I feel that I was controlled or censured.

I began by telling the pupils who I was, where I came from and what I did for my living. I gave them my view of the situation and what I would like to happen in Germany. My audience was absolutely engaged. The pupils asked me hundreds of questions mostly about my everyday life and about items like fashion, pop stars and the meaning of slang they had heard on the radio. However, in every lesson sooner or later the question arose: "Why can't we get bananas?"

Bananas were and still are the Germans' favourite fruit. Millions of babies have been fed mashed bananas and as toddlers have squashed pieces of banana into soft furnishings. The lack of bananas in the DDR was something everybody felt deeply and it encapsulated the many questions about all kinds of shortages.

In answering this question, I tried to remind the students that bananas grew in tropical countries and those countries wanted to be paid in hard currency which the DDR Mark was not. To obtain hard currency the DDR had to export their products to Western countries and there they had to compete in a capitalist market which was difficult with their kind of productivity. It was low in comparison because they did not exploit people the way the capitalist system did. It was the price they paid for having full employment. In the end every imported banana would mean a shortage of other imported goods and that was the dilemma. From there it was only a short step to the question as to what made a currency a 'hard' currency and thus we landed in the middle of macro-economic theories. I really had to pull all my knowledge and wit together to formulate sensible answers.

One teacher afterwards remarked - and she was quite offended - that she had taught the same subject just a week previously but nobody seemed to have listened to her. I believe that what the pupils wanted above all else was somebody they could trust. Already at that age they had the slightly cynical attitude that everything they were presented with in school and in other state-run organisations could not really be true, at least it could not be the complete truth. I might have appeared authentic to them, perhaps only because my language was totally untouched by the official-speak they were so accustomed to.

Ute and I went home and congratulated ourselves on a wonderful and interesting teaching experiment. The next morning, I travelled to Dresden for a few days. Therefore, I did not have to bear the brunt of the storm that erupted following my day in school. Whoever was involved in the affair was questioned by the authorities; the headmaster nearly lost his job and was heavily reprimanded. In the end every school, every factory, every office in the area had to sign a pledge never ever to allow West Germans on their premises again without explicit and written permission from the Party (SED = United Socialist Party Germany).

I was devastated when I heard about it because I realised I had caused so much trouble to so many people. But Ute's headmaster sent me a reassuring message telling me that he knew exactly what he was doing, that he was close to retiring and that *they* could not do much harm to him anyway. He still believed that his pupils had had one of the best days in their school life, not to mention the sensation at finding themselves in the middle of a political turmoil without being the ones to be blamed for it.

As it turned out there were a number of pupils whose parents worked for the "Staatssicherheitsdienst/Stasi" (secret services). When those children went home and quite innocently spoke about their exciting day in school, the shocked parents detected 'the enemy within' and alerted the authorities.

18. How not to become a spy

The general attitude towards the Stasi was ambivalent to say the least. Officially, those in the Secret Services were heroes who defended their socialist society on the 'hidden front'. Like the army they were highly praised for their bravery and their loyalty. On the other hand, people realised that the first to be spied on were they themselves and, by being faithful to socialism, Stasi informers might find themselves in the position of betraying their next of kin, their friends or their colleagues. As individuals they were thought to wield a lot of power, at least more power than the average citizen and thus you would not readily fall out with one of them. There was no right of appeal against being blacklisted, no matter how much it might have interfered with all your hopes and plans. What subject you were allowed to study, what job you got and whether you would be promoted in your job, always also depended on the report the Stasi gave about your behaviour and attitudes.

There was an obvious difference between the official staff and the informal informers of the secret services. The officials did their jobs as policemen would. They saw themselves as organisers and planners of public safety and were trained for what they did. It was the informal informants who were much more despised because what they did was denunciation of people who were often their nearest and dearest. Later on, after the "Wende", which was brought about by numerous groups of people who were willing to risk a lot to change the system, it was revealed that in some cases the number of informal informers in these groups had been enormous. They had no idea who else was an informer and to appear believable each one tried to behave even more radical than the next person and so help change to come even faster. Thus, it could be said that the peaceful revolution in the DDR was partly due to the zealous sense of duty and the creativity of the secret service and its individual members.

At one time Ute and her husband had made friends with the parents of one of Ute's pupils and it turned out that the pupil's parents were both Stasi officers. I was under the impression that the initiative for the friendship rather came from the other side and that Ute and Eberhard found it difficult not to reciprocate. It was not the done thing to annoy people like this, but I might have been wrong.

As official members of the secret service these people were not to have any kind of contact with Westerners, which meant that although I was told about them I was never to meet them. So, while one of them was in the house I had to stay away. This was not because their loyalty would have been endangered by any contact with Westerners; it was because of the fear that after returning to West Germany I could and would identify them to "our" secret services. There was a rumour that every DDR citizen who had been allowed to travel to the West was debriefed afterwards and obviously they perceived it would be the same the other way around.

While we would normally scrupulously avoid each other, on one occasion our timing did not work. Or could it have been that curiosity was stronger than caution? The pupil's mother had announced her visit. I went for a walk and returned at the agreed time. However, when I entered the house the woman was still there. We suddenly faced each other in the hallway. There stood a rather young blonde woman who stared at me with wide open eyes, as if she wanted to take in every little detail and keep the memory for ever.

I said:" Hello". She did not answer and Ute had to transmit her message by stating that it was bad enough that we had met, but that her friend would not break her promise and speak to me.

Thus, an absurd kind of acknowledgement happened between us. I addressed her and she gave her replies to Ute. It lasted only a minute or two and then Ute indicated that I should get out of the way and step into a room so that her friend could pass by and leave the house. Afterwards even Ute was quite sure that her friend had delayed her departure on purpose to have a good look at a West German person. I have to admit I did feel a bit like an exotic animal and thought the whole thing to be absolutely weird.

Throughout her life Ute had a strong sense of duty and worked very hard to improve her skills and to find new and creative ways of teaching. Eventually her efforts were recognised and she was invited to partake in a scientific research program, as she proudly told me in one of her letters. Thus, she became a member of a small team, where they discussed educational questions. From time to time she was asked to write down her ideas, research literature or report about what was going on in her school. This went on for some time and as it happens private matters crept into the official exchanges. One day Ute was asked if she had any West German relations and she told her partners about me. They were very interested and expressed a wish to meet me the next time I would visit her. Ute asked me whether that would be okay and I had no reason to say no. I wrote to her that I would be happy to meet her colleagues.

When I eventually arrived in Erfurt, Ute was much less enthusiastic. Very soon she admitted that meanwhile she was pretty convinced that it was the secret service who was behind the whole research program and that she was deeply disappointed she had been deceived by being kept busy with so called researches while at the end of the day all these men had wanted was to make contact with me, her cousin. She was sure she was not supposed to warn me but she had done it so that I could make up my own mind. She left it to me how I wanted to react to this approach even if it meant that her prospects could be endangered if I refused any contact from the very start. Of course, I did not want to do any harm and I was curious. In a fighting mood I told her:

"Let them come!"

One day two men arrived at the house. Firstly, the four of us had a cup of coffee and made polite small talk. After a while Ute cleared the table and disappeared into the kitchen leaving me alone with them. Quickly the discussion became more focussed on political and social questions. I did not feel frightened at all. There was no reason for me to please them and so I told them quite bluntly what I felt and thought. Perhaps I had expected that they would be as easily frustrated as the political agitator I had angered all these years ago, and that they would give me good reason to excuse myself and terminate the discussion, however they were made of sterner stuff.

I was totally surprised when they agreed to most of what I said and even volunteered more and harsher criticism of their own system. They seemed to be quite open about mistakes and absurdities that re-occurred again and again. Equally surprising was that they were fairly open about who they were. Quickly they admitted to being Stasi officers. They explained to me that the black and white picture of what the Stasi did was only half the truth. Another of their tasks which normally was not mentioned was to help improve the general situation by indicating what had gone wrong and to help find solutions.

It was certainly true that in all my time in the DDR I had never come upon people who called a spade a spade as these two did. They seemed to have no illusion and did not practise any kind of the usual double-think. They were socialists and wanted to help to build a free and just society. They were far from this goal, they admitted, and the way was long and difficult. They needed all the help they could get by meeting people who would not seek any personal advantage by repeating to them the propaganda they themselves had invented. Therefore, they told me they were eager to make contact with people who were outspoken, who had a clear view and the analytical ability to formulate what for many others would only be vague gut feelings.

There it was! That was what they wanted from me! In the real world I was a nobody, I was of no interest to anybody. What I thought or felt made no difference whatsoever. Suddenly there were people who gave me the feeling that my ideas had some relevance and could eventually help to change the world for the better. What a challenge! What a seduction! One had to admit, they were very good psychologists and experienced in identifying the week spots of their targets.

The men invited me to visit Berlin (East Berlin, their capital, of course) and I accepted. The next day they drove me to Berlin and put me up for a night at the best hotel in town right beside the Alexander place. They continued to be interested and courteous and pampered me in every possible way. When they brought me back to Erfurt I was half convinced it was my duty to contribute to world peace by letting them have some nuggets of my twenty-something wisdom. I told Ute all about my trip and so that we could communicate by letter, which probably would be censured, we developed our own private code for the Stasi men and their and our respective fate.

As far as Ute was concerned these men disappeared from her life as suddenly as they had appeared, thus strengthening her belief that she was no more than a tool. It did not take long until using our secret code I informed her that I had pretty soon awoken from the dream of becoming an important mover and shaker of history. I had touched the hard ground of reality again and realised how good had been the bait they had thrown in my direction. However, I was not as stupid as that. Then I wrote a letter to the address they had given me with the following content: "Thank you for your kind invitation to become a spy, but no thank you. I realised I am not agent material at all. I do not mind doing my bit however limited for world peace but I prefer to do it in the open." And that was the end of that.

Years later when I entrusted Michael, my future husband, with my Stasi adventures he surprised me with a similar story. He too had family relations in Saxonia-Anhalt whom he used to visit on a regular basis. The same kind of interested visitors appeared and tried to establish contact with him. They tried to hook him with books. If you were acquainted with Michael you would understand how fitting that bait was. He too declined as politely as he could. It might easily have been that every West German student who ventured into the East sooner or later was targeted by the Stasi. I did tell you that we were not exceptional, didn't I?

My relationship with Ute continued as usual. I was interested to hear about her family, about her little daughter, about her job and about the successes or disappointments they had had while trying to maintain their house under the usual regime of shortages of tools and materials.

The sister of a school friend of mine had married into the DDR and my school friend told me how her sister wanted to order a bath tub. As usual she was asked to sign a waiting list on which she was number 300 or so.

'So how many bathtubs come in each month?' she asked.

'One or two a year.' was the answer.

That was normal unless you had special contacts. Realistically, much of what you needed you had to find on the exchange market. Fortunately, Ute's husband Eberhard was placed quite comfortably as he worked as a locksmith for a large nursery and garden centre and thus had access to various ranges of desirable articles. And yet I knew that it was an uphill struggle to do all he wanted to do in the old house and in the garden.

19. While we were separated

One day I received a letter that was different from all the hundreds Ute had written to me. She and Eberhard had thought long and hard about their future, she wrote. They very much wanted to see more of the world and not just the handful of places to which they were allowed to travel. Their greatest wish was to live abroad for a while with the possibility of a return to Erfurt. There were only a few legal ways to leave the DDR. You either had to become a top athlete, a member of the diplomatic corps or a development aid worker in the Third World where the DDR had started their own projects. As it probably was too late for the first and their education was not right for the second they had applied for the third and had received a positive answer as their combination of teacher and master craftsman seemed to be very desirable.

A probable destination would be French speaking Africa, where several countries had established diplomatic relations with the DDR. Before Ute and her family could go they had to undergo training and language courses. But there was another condition: They had to prove their loyalty to their state by severing all ties with West Germans or any other Westerners completely. That meant, we could no longer remain in contact! Would I understand her motives? Would I be angry with her or disappointed?

Obviously, I was very sad. Ute had been a part of

my life for such a long time. I could hardly imagine a life without her. But who was I to judge her? I could travel wherever I wanted as long as I could pay for it. To me the world had always been open and I had enjoyed as much of it as I could. I was sad but I understood her perfectly well.

And I kept my promise. During fourteen long years I did not try to contact her although I always felt the loss. The really enraging thing about it - which cannot be put right as no-one can turn back the clock - was that all our sacrifices were in vain! The authorities never allowed them to leave the country. Not in all those years when they kept her in suspense, controlled her every move and kept her busy with ever new tasks. However, we did not know that when we parted in 1975, I hoped for her that she would be able to fulfil her dreams and she was full of hope as well.

Life went on. Of course, it did. I met my future husband Michael in 1977 and a year later we moved in together. At that time, he was doing a PhD in physics. We were both interested in the emerging problems of atomic energy and alternative energies. We joined a university seminar which dealt with those problems. It developed into one of the best groups we were ever part of. What was special about this group was that undergraduates, postgraduates and lecturers worked side by side on equal terms on a concept of how one could run a city like Munich (1,2 million inhabitants) without atomic energy but by saving energy and by the intelligent use and combination of alternative and conventional energy sources. It took us four years to complete our researches – none of it being funded by anybody - but in the end our concept was so detailed and so scientifically sound that the city council established a special enquiry into our results and took a number of our suggestions on board. Our group, together with many similar initiatives at that time in Germany, was one of many nuclei for what afterwards emerged as the Green Party and the Peace Movement. One of the professors, Hans Peter Duerr, who was one of the founders of the seminar and a father figure to most of us, was given the Alternative Nobel Prize for this engagement in the question of survival of the environment and human society.

After Michael had finished his PhD he got his first job in the Ruhr area. This is a highly industrial area in the Northwest of Germany which developed with coal mining and the steel industry in the 19th century. Now they were in the middle of the process to convert to other fields of production because international competition made it more and more difficult for the national heavy industry.

We were married in 1982 and moved to a small village on the edge of this area. Shortly afterwards the local newspaper published an invitation for a local meeting of likeminded people. We attended and, consequently, we can call ourselves founder members of the local branch of the Green Party. Not long after this first meeting both of us were elected to the local council.

It was a fascinating moment. We were the first generation of Greens in any council. Prejudices were widespread. The establishment imagined wild hordes of unwashed work-shy taking over their sacred chamber. Instead amongst the seven of us there was the wife of a well-respected local GP, a physicist with a Ph.D., a social worker, one member of the civil service, a decent married couple etc. They just did not know what to make of us and secretly discussed all kind of emergencies in case we misbehaved, which we did *not*.

Unknown to me at about the same time Ute was elected onto the Erfurt town council as a member of the LDPD (Liberaldemokratische Partei Deutschlands = Liberal Democratic Party). Although for a long time she was pressured to apply to become a member of the all-powerful SED (Sozialistische Einheitspartei Deutschland = United Socialist Party) she had preferred to join another party if she had to join one at all.

The SED was a forced union of the former SPD (Social Democratic Party) with the former KPD (Communist Party). It was the ruling power in the DDR. However, it was never the only legal party. Traditionally and much older than the DDR were the CDU (Christian Democratic Party) and the LPD (Liberal Democratic Party, later LDPD), the latter initially even in explicit opposition to the SED. Under soviet influence, two more parties were formed, the NDPD (National Democratic Party) and the BPD (farmers' party).

The idea was that all parts of society should be represented. That did not imply that there were independent. Of course, they had to submit to the over-all dictate of the proletariat. They were forced into what was called "The National Front" under the direction of the SED. Nevertheless, the LDPD was considered the one to provide at least a bit of opposition. Some old liberal traditions survived underground and thus this party was the choice of many of the intelligentsia. However, there was a certain price to pay. As a teacher you could join the LDPD but you could never then become a headmaster. The best you could achieve was to be promoted to assistant head teacher but the top person had to be a Comrade.

So, unknown to each other, we both, Ute and I, ended up sitting on a council for a small and pestering opposition party. Local politics as I witnessed it was exactly as Billy Voter imagines it to be. The real influence of the individual politician can only be overestimated. Ninety-five percent of real power lies with the civil service. All a leading party can do to enforce their line of thinking is to advance party loyal civil servants into positions of influence within the administration and then hope that the proposed politics will be according to the party manifesto. Civil servants are trained to do their job. They have the facts or at least they have the time and resources to collect relevant information. They know where the money is and where it should be. If they do not like a political initiative they will easily find a law or a directive or some financial problem that will make it impossible to follow up the idea. They are there for a working life-time making sure that they do not become stressed out or made redundant. Compared to their position, elected council members are very much like a travelling circus coming into town. When they are really engaged they might ruffle a few feathers but soon things calm down again and life goes on as it always did.

The truth is: civil servants are the professionals, and you, as an elected member of the council, are nothing more than a well-meaning amateur. The administration has the capacity to research their objectives properly. You are confronted at short notice with the draft for a resolution or with a decision to spend money. You might have some gut feeling but in the majority of cases you are not in the position to work out and argue for a proper alternative. It probably would be love's labour lost anyway because party members will always vote along party lines, although in private conversation they might admit that in their heart of hearts they would have favoured another party's suggestion.

The way politicians dealt with each other was weird and sometimes frightening. I was accustomed to people being friendly to my face and talking badly behind my back. In politics I had to learn it was the other way around. In public heaps of dirt were emptied over your head by the political opponent. Afterwards in a private conversation they would tell you how much they liked what you suggested and how happy they would have been to vote for you if only...

Or you heard through the grape vine that the Social Democrats would readily give their back teeth if you would switch to their party only an hour after they had denounced you publicly as a halfwit and a terrorist. No wonder alcohol plays a huge part in political life because not only does it help politicians to digest the aggression but by being drunk he or she can dare to be friendly even with the political opponent. Booze is always an accepted excuse if you are found out for fraternising.

Due to our electoral success they had to allow us to chair one committee. Thus, I was elected chairperson of the committee that dealt with questions of public health. I was the only Green member on the committee, the only woman and the youngest member by far. And yet all these middle-aged men, many of them professionals within the health system, had to obey my orders and when I thought they had exhausted a theme I was able to cut them short. Which was nice!

I remember one occasion. My parents came for a visit and of course they wanted to see their politician-daughter in action. It was good luck that while they were with us there was a committee meeting. There would be one part which was open to the public whilst due to regulations I would have to exclude the audience for the last ten minutes. I had explained this to my parents, thus, when I had to ask the public to leave, they - the only representatives of the public in that late hour – rose and left the chamber. Then I addressed the committee by saying: "Now, that I have sent my parents away, we may continue with...."

Sensation! Members of the Green Party have parents!?! Who might even be proud of what their children are up to!?! After the meeting my parents who were waiting for me outside found themselves surrounded by committee members who congratulated them on their daughter who did such a great job as a chairperson. One of the senior doctors even kissed her hand, my mother giggling confessed to me later.

When I took the chair, the health committee was not considered to be of great importance. Otherwise the SPD which was in overall control of the council would never have given away this position. But then the nuclear accident in Chernobyl happened and suddenly I and my committee were at the centre of all the attention and at least in the region I became a household name.

After the reactor catastrophe Michael and I were very much in demand. For nearly a year we were constantly invited to give talks and to take part in public debates. Michael as a physicist who had worked with nuclear materials helped people to understand what had happened, what radioactivity was and what kind of danger it presented. My role was more to talk about the wider field of energy supply. What a society needed and how it could be provided; what kind of sources there were and how long they would last; and of course, the fundamental question:

could we manage without nuclear energy.

Subsequently I was elected or rather pushed into running as the local candidate for the Green Party at the next general election. In Germany we have two votes, one "first past the post", where we elect one person, and a second, a proportional vote, where we vote for party lists. Although the Green Party might be successful via party lists there was never a chance for a Green person to be elected "first past the post", but as my local friends needed a figurehead they thought I would be stupid enough and do nicely, thank you very much. Today I can state proudly that I was quite a sensation within an otherwise boring campaign. Again, I was the only female amongst men. Often together with the other three candidates of the main parties I toured the area from podium to podium. After a while I realised that the others had started to imitate my way of speaking. "Renate says..." became the trade mark of the campaign. In the end I got more first votes for me as a person, than the Green party got second votes, although the party did alright as well. So, there you are!

Now let us talk about corruption. In (local) politics it is very much alive and kicking. It is not so much that money changes hands, although even that probably happens from time to time. It is knowledge that is power and those well informed attract all kinds of attention and receive offers to exchange their knowledge with others in similar positions of influence. Remarkably enough those within the system would never consider themselves as being corrupt although they very naturally would always take in account their and their friends' interests in whatever decision they have to take.

As I have experienced myself it is quite difficult not to profit from a public position. As a member of council, you just have certain privileges. A lot of doors opened with ease which normally would be tightly shut for the average citizen. On more than one occasion I was thought to be in the know and well connected - whether it was true or not – so I received extra attention and additional information. People always want to network so that what first might have been fiction – that I possessed special information and influence - suddenly became a reality. For a few years within a certain political context I was somebody who was well known. This was shown most clearly by those who cited me when discussing politics.

The influence that we as a small newly founded party had was probably more in the modification of general attitudes than factual changes. We definitely brought the younger generation into local politics and changed the way people communicated. It was always quite fascinating to see how council members woke up from their slumber when one of us started to speak as they knew that we would do our best to avoid political jargon and would just say what we thought. In his decade Joschka Fischer, the former Green foreign secretary (1998-2005), who started his political life in Frankfurt as a street fighter and squatter, was one of the best liked politicians in Germany, as people experience him as straightforward and utterly honest.

An important moment during the annual cycle was when the following year's budget was being discussed. On this occasion it was not only the financial planning which was discussed. It was also a general debate on what had happened over the previous period. Again, it fell to me to give the first ever Green budget speech. I finished by telling the members of the other parties how strange that first year had been for us and how difficult it was to get accustomed to the fact that many of them did not only despise our political statements but also seemed to hate us personally. There was a long and dismayed silence and then people started to hurry forwards to tell me how much they felt exactly the same and how much they had suffered under this artificial hostility prescribed – or so they thought - by their party loyalty.

My time as a council member was interesting and I learnt a lot. I will never be afraid of administrations anymore because I had so much opportunity to study the psyche of those working these systems. But when after five years the next local elections came up I was glad that for professional reasons we had to move to another town and thus there could be no pressure on me to run for office once more.

For Ute the limits of what she could achieve as a member of a council were even more obvious. In a top to bottom system, as it was the rule in the DDR, decisions were taken at the highest level and then handed down to local level as orders that had to be fulfilled and not questioned. All that could be decided on council level was, how best to put general directions into local practice. Most of Ute's political life consisted of listening to people explaining other people's ideas and how socialism would be reached inexorably by the new directive.

Ute later told me how she landed herself in real trouble once when, after one session, she made a personal remark to another member of the council. The subject of the general discussion had been about the money the state collected with the forced exchange of money by Western visitors to which I related before. All Ute had said, in what she thought was a private conversation, was that she felt astounded that there were no concessions for students or pensioners. As far as she understood and had always been told that in the West those two groups were really hard up and could hardly afford a decent living and certainly not the daily exchange of 10, - DM. But there was not such a thing as a private conversation. Her remarks were reported to the authorities immediately. She had to appear before a panel and was accused of jeopardising the basis of socialism and the right of the state to raise its international profile with her critical and cynical attitude. She was informed that if she did not change her ways immediately and profoundly she could no longer be a teacher. Even her role as a mother could be questioned. This meant that there was the threat that her daughter would be put into care. Of course, Ute submitted to whatever was asked of her, denounced herself publicly in front of the whole council for her errors and pledged total agreement with whatever the Party (SED) would decide.

20. The Big Thaw

There seemed to be no end to the cold war stalemate between East and West. However, one step after the other was taken to slowly ease the tension. In 1973 the Conference for Security and Cooperation in Europe (CSCE) was established in Helsinki as a platform where all European States (except Albania) met to give themselves some rules to keep the peace, improve economic cooperation and obtain humanitarian improvements for the peoples in the Soviet Block. In some East European countries subsequently, civil rights movements sprang from these CSCE protocols, among them Poland's Solidarnosc, a new and independent trade union, which was formed and survived although the political and military pressure was enormous.

In 1985 a man named Mikhail Gorbachev was elected General Secretary of the Central Committee of the Communist Party of the USSR. He initiated moves to change the world that none of us could ever have imagined. Dissatisfaction which was suppressed for so long suddenly erupted. People stopped being afraid and remembered how much power could be wielded by masses of peaceful and determined protesters.

In the DDR groups formed, often under the umbrella of the protestant churches. People took an interest in local or global questions. They began to dispute controversial issues instead of simply toeing the party line. They acted absolutely peaceful and by doing so they disarmed the power of state and party. Those in power tried to defend the status quo by sending in police or soldiers. But – as it had happened in Czechoslovakia twenty years before – the armed troops found it difficult to shoot at people who were obviously unarmed and did nothing worse than to suggest having a discussion about what went wrong.

In Erfurt, as Ute told me later, the spark which brought thousands onto the streets was a plan to demolish an old part of the town. Although in the DDR a few outstanding buildings were carefully preserved, saving historical sites was not considered an essential for society. Such buildings represented another time and the sooner society rid itself of them - and the memories of the past - the sooner the country could be turned into a socialist paradise.

Now Erfurt was and is a town full of old buildings and the people were proud of their historical inheritance. The area in question, the Andreas Quarter, was basically a mediaeval poor men's dwelling, small houses lining narrow alleys. Years of systematic neglect had made it virtually uninhabitable and the council's plan was to pull it down and to replace it with the usual high-rise prefabricated blocks that were so typical of the DDR's urban landscape.

It had happened a hundred times before and often with even more deserving buildings. Castles, churches and old houses had been destroyed all over the Republic to make room for those blocks. Sometimes historical buildings were destroyed and not replaced only because they were remnants of another historical period.

However, now the climate had changed. People did not wish to live prefabricated lives any more. They ceased to see anything positive in uniformity. They felt that by destroying a whole quarter of the old historic Erfurt another piece of the town's soul would be lost for ever. Thousands of the citizens of Erfurt formed human chains around the Andreas Quarter again and again whenever it was necessary to protect these houses.

It was dangerous. Shadows of public protests which had been silenced by force loomed large. Still people were overwhelmed by how good it felt to be there, together with so many others. All of a sudden, they began to talk. They started by telling each other, what was wrong with their lives, and soon proceeded to suggesting how things could be improved. Last but not least they witnessed the authorities, the politicians, the police, the military in total confusion as those in power had no idea how to react.

In China at the same time a protest movement was brutally crushed. The pictures went around the world and many, including Ute, thought that they might be the next in line. However, the worldwide outcry after Tiananmen Square was so profound that those in power in the DDR staggered between their primal instinct to squash every resistance from its start, and the widespread insight that so much had gone wrong in their system and had been going wrong for such a long time, that change just had to happen.

In more than one moment during these exciting months it was down to individuals to take far-reaching decisions as events were evolving fast. No general orientation was coming down from the top as lower charges were so accustomed to. Very often individuals in the frontline decided against piling guilt on their heads and refrained from opening fire on their compatriots.

We in West Germany witnessed all this with amazement and rising hopes. I remember us sitting around the kitchen table, glued to the radio, listening to the new DDR head of party and state Egon Krenz giving his first official speech. How we tried to decipher among all the party jargon, what would really be new and what would really change. We took him seriously although history did not and in the end his rule was no more than a foot note. Still at that time our hopes were so modest!

Sometime late in the summer of 1989 Michael had a lively discussion with Scottish friends (for many years we have owned a second home on the west coast of Scotland). They asked him whether he thought the Berlin Wall would ever come down. Michael is and always has been an optimist and so he explained that he was sure that one day it would happen. But, he said, he doubted it would happen in our life-time. Had I been there I would have totally agreed with him and so would the vast majority of Germans.

Because of this general belief a lot of people in the DDR had lost any hope that things would ever change. In huge numbers they now began to use every possible method for leaving their country. Hungary had started to relax their border fortifications and many used the opportunity to cross the border into Austria illegally but at least they no longer ran the risk of losing their lives. The DDR reacted by restricting visas to Hungary to essential cases only.

Next some people used their tourist visas for Czechoslovakia to seek asylum in the embassy of the Federal Republic of Germany in Prague. After a few days the embassy was full but every day still more and more people were climbing the fences and the walls. We saw dramatic pictures on TV: whole families making it over the high walls, parents throwing their children over the fence first and then scrambling over themselves while being pushed from behind and pulled from above. Half-heartedly the Czech police tried to block the streets leading to the embassy but the roadblocks were just run over by the masses finding their way to the wall and fences.

There were thousands in the embassy. It must have looked like a refugee camp. Living conditions must have been dire. Diplomats of all involved countries worked day and night to find a solution while still the refugees came in droves. Eventually the DDR had to give in. All those in the embassy were allowed to abandon DDR citizenship and travel to West Germany but the authorities insisted that they had to travel through the territory of the DDR.

That was probably one of the greatest mistakes those in power in the DDR ever committed. The refugees were packed in a train and off they went. It was like a triumphal procession. While on DDR territory, other people desperately tried to climb onto the train. The West German embassy in Prague was stormed by another few thousand refugees immediately, in the conviction that they would be on the next train to West Germany. There had to be another solution.

It was two months after that famous discussion Michael had had with our Scottish friends. We were back in Germany. After a long day in the office I was just having a late soaking in the bath tub when Michael suddenly shouted from the living room - and I remember every word as if it had been yesterday - 'If I understand correctly what just has been said on TV, the Wall is open!' It was the evening of the ninth of November 1989.

What he had watched on TV was a press conference Günther Schabowski was giving on behalf of the SED Polit Bureau and the DDR government. He stated that from in future citizens of the DDR could leave from and re-enter into their country directly from West Germany without having to travel via third countries. They would be able to do so whenever they wished. All they had to do was to obtain a visa. Asked when this regulation would come in force and whether it included Berlin, he had no specific instructions and so he improvised and said that he believed it was from that moment on and that it included Berlin as well.

Minutes later in East Berlin thousands of people rushed to the few transit points within the Wall and demanded to be allowed through. The poor border guards in the absence of any superiors and without any orders or advice eventually gave way and that is what happened during that historical night.

Miracles happen seldom but one happened that night. One of the most moving scenes I saw later–on TV was that of an elderly woman who stood in East Berlin front of the Brandenburg Gate which was still no-mans-land and heavily guarded, crying and begging the soldiers to allow her to walk up to the gate once in her life. The soldiers although they turned away from the crying woman seemed utterly shaken. The next moment they had opened the roadblock and one of them offered his arm to the old lady to guide her through the gate to the other side and back, both of them shaking with emotions.

To tell you the truth we had not a clue. The news had not sunk in at all. The very idea of an open border was so totally absurd. We thought that there would be a lengthy and spiteful bureaucratic process and occasionally an individual would arrive from East Germany. So, we went to bed.

Only on the next morning when we saw people dancing on the Wall did we start to understand that something unbelievable must have happened during the night. We rushed to the living room, turned on the TV and there it was: People dancing on the Wall!

Streams of people flowing freely over the checkpoints, crying and shouting: "This is unbelievable!" and waving champagne bottles. Those thousands were cheered by equally exited West Berliners who had come out after watching the same TV stations and hearing the very same words. West Berliners lined the route to greet each and every one, they knocked on or threw flowers on arriving cars, hugged total strangers, invited them to pubs and bars or into their homes for a drink – of course East Berliners did not have the 'right' kind of money – they had what must have been the ultimate street party – every German who wasn't there will be envious for the rest of his life, I can tell you.

Michael and I sat in front of the TV clutching our mugs and crying into our tea. It was one of the most important moments of our lives and we realised it there and then. It came as a shock to us that for the first time in our lives we could freely admit how much the existence of the Wall had really hurt.

It had hurt always, this monstrous building, that Wall through a city and through a country. It hurt so much you had to suppress the pain mentally or you would not have been able to live with it. Now it looked like a gigantic slain dragon. And the fact that those who danced on the beast were totally harmless young folks in their everyday clothes, unarmed and peaceful, themselves surprised by their own daring, looking down on the heavily armed equally young soldiers who did not know what to do and thus rather did nothing, made it so much sweeter.

And then of course there was Ute. I had thought of her a lot during the previous months and now with events rushing along at this unbelievable speed I could not imagine that any attempt to get into contact with her could harm her any longer. Everybody knew that something had come to an end and even if we could not foresee that soon afterwards the DDR would cease to exist, already then, we felt that whatever the new order would be it would have new rules.

Therefore, I sat down to write a letter to the old address – the house that always was. There had been some information dripping through via other relatives like the sad news of her mother's death from cancer. Therefore, I was pretty sure I would have heard about it had she given up the house and moved away.

To write this letter was quite some task. How do you tell the story of fourteen years without unnerving the addressee with page upon page if you are not even sure whether a letter will be welcome at all? Was there still some kind of censorship and who would read the letter - besides Ute - and misunderstand it?

The answer to my letter came as fast as one could wish for. Ute gave me the same kind of compact report of what had happened during the last years. Then she explained that due to her mother's illness they possessed what still was a precious commodity in the DDR at that time. They had a private telephone! Would I like to try to call her?

I could not wait to hear her voice. I wanted to tell her how happy I was about all and everything and how much I would love to see her as soon as possible. I sat down and dialled that wonderful number. The international line was engaged. I pushed the redial button. The line was engaged. I pushed the redial button. Engaged. I pushed the redial button. Beep beep beep...

There were only a few lines open between the two German states. Again, the DDR had only allowed a minimum as they had no interest in easing contacts between East and West and furthermore the Stasi was supposed to listen into every telephone call. Therefore, telephone traffic had always been slow. As you knew that somebody else could be listening, normally you made a telephone call only for absolutely crucial reasons and you concentrated on essentials.

Thus, it was nothing new that to get a connection might take some time. But now with all that euphoria there was no holding back. Whatever had frightened people before about speaking openly on the telephone was blown away, although at the time the Stasi was still alive and kicking. People talked and talked on the telephone and thus calls took longer and longer and who ever wanted to place a call had to wait even longer.

I had to dial and to redial for 18 (eighteen!) hours. Can you imagine what your finger does after pushing buttons for such a long time? Thank God for the redial button! After a while you simply can't stop pushing the very same buttons again and again, but you have totally forgotten why you are doing it in the first place.

Michael went to bed and got up again in the morning and still I was sitting there, pushing my buttons. Suddenly I received a different tone, a ringing tone. I could not believe what I was hearing.

Then a female voice I immediately recognised answered.

"Ute?" I asked cautiously, although I was sure I had the right number.

"No," was the answer, "This is Susanne, Ute's daughter."

Susanne, the lioness, I had last seen, when she was just grown out of the toddler stage! And now she was a young woman and her voice was so very much like her mother's that it was mind-blowing.

I explained who I was. I said I was sure she could not remember me but I remembered her well. She said not at all, she knew exactly who I was and she even had the feeling she remembered me from years back. When she called for her mother I could hear her squealing with joy.

By the time Ute came to the telephone I had difficulties in coping with my emotions. Thus, although there was so much to say the conversation was awkward and we probably were both a bit incoherent. I remember that we talked for a while about the fact that she had a telephone at all and how sad it was that she was only allowed telephone access because of her mother's illness. She then told me that the bureaucratic process had taken so long that her mother had already died before the telephone was eventually installed.

I know, I know, we should have made better use of the precious time but that is how it was. At least we were able to set a date for a first visit. It was agreed that Michael and I would travel to Erfurt first. I put down the receiver. I was shaking from head to toe.

21. Picking up the thread

Soon people could travel freely in both directions but still two different states existed with their separate sovereignty. The physical border had lost some of its horrors but it was still there and manned. Only a handful of crossing points existed and although some of the concrete obstacles had been moved it took us hours to get through when we drove to Erfurt for the first time.

Of course, nobody had been prepared for so much traffic in both directions. For forty years there had been no reason whatsoever to maintain or widen the roads while on both sides of the border a wide strip of land had lain virtually empty. In the East that strip of land had been cleared forcefully. People who still lived or worked there needed special permits to enter the zone. The area west of this impenetrable border had become the poorest and least developed of the Federal Republic. Although investment programs were installed droves of people had moved away in search of better working opportunities elsewhere.

In both countries North-South had become the main direction of traffic while East-West axes were neglected. North-South was where new motorways had been built and railway tracks had been laid down to cope with the ever-higher demands. Now suddenly there was an unstoppable East-West flow and the infrastructure could only break down under the new and sudden burden.

I had seen the structure of the border on a few occasions, first when I went to Erfurt by train and later when I drove to West Berlin with my car. There were barbed-wire fences, electrically charged fences, strips of land with trip wires that would alert the border guard if touched or even worse, trigger automatic gun fire, strips that were sanded so that one could detect footprints of those who tried to flee. There were strips where dogs patrolled, strips where soldiers patrolled and watchtowers. This part of the system was up to 500 yards deep. Next was an area where only the presence of military personnel was allowed. After this the five-kilometre zone where people needed the above-mentioned special permits to enter.

The average citizen of the DDR never had the chance to see those fortifications with their own eyes. They were stopped long before they could approach the physical border. They were indoctrinated that it was there to protect them against any aggression from the West. Seeing the thing in the flesh you realised that this was utter nonsense. The majority of people in the DDR had no idea how obvious and aggressive this thing called "Peace Frontier" was first and foremost directed against themselves. The way it was constructed it could hardly have stopped a tank. But it did stop people from fleeing the country. This is what it was supposed to do and this is why it was built in the first place.

After hours of stop and go we eventually

reached Erfurt. Now I had never arrived there by car and my last visit was fourteen years ago. I had no idea where we would enter the town and of course I had no road map. Maps were generally hard to come by in the DDR. They were supposed to constitute a danger should they fall into the hands of the enemy. Even those that existed were unreliable. Parts, which were considered security sensitive, were simply left out or painted over. However, some areas were omitted not for security reasons but because they wished to maintain ignorance among their own citizens. Thus, the restricted areas where the 'Bonzen' (bigwigs) had their villas and hunting grounds appeared on no map.

Ute had given me a rough description which relied heavily on the possibility that I basically knew my way around. And that was exactly what happened. When we entered the town, I recognised the very road on which we were driving. I knew that Ute lived somewhere off that road and all I then had to do was to identify the right turn. It was awesome. I knew exactly where I was.

Eventually we had parked the car and walked up to the front door. It was still the house I always knew. Later I would appreciate how much Eberhard had done to keep it in good shape, but the first overwhelming feeling was that nothing had changed at all. The door opened and there they were: Ute and Eberhard. We embraced. We laughed. No, we did not cry. We are both rather unsentimental in the sense that we don't mind shedding a few tears when a weepy is on TV but mostly put on a brave face when in real life there were good reasons for emotions to run high.

Of course, we were extremely excited. Almost certainly Ute and I talked simultaneously. We can do this, you know, to the constant amusement of our husbands. What seemed like an absolute miracle – and then perhaps it was not - was that we conversed as if we had stop speaking only a day ago. The way in which we always understood each other still worked after all these years.

There was a lot to tell and a lot of catching up to do. Michael was an unknown factor to both of them. Much later Ute confessed that before they met him they were a bit apprehensive about him being a professor of physics. But whatever intimidation they might have anticipated it vanished fast and soon Eberhard and Michael were lost in big boy's toys talk about tools and cars, stereos and videos.

Later Susanne joined us together with her then fiancé. He was a nice guy but it seemed to me as if events were about to repeat themselves. Susanne - as her mother twenty years before – had this anxiousness that if she did not tie down a husband before her twentieth birthday she would be regarded as having been left on the shelf.

In the end the historical turn-around might have saved her from bigger disappointment. The young people enjoyed their newly won freedom. Suddenly a wider choice of professional future was open to them, not to mention a whole world waiting to be explored. After they had experienced some of those new opportunities the couple realised that their ideas about how they wanted to live had more and more grown apart and they decided to split up. But this was in the future. When we first met them we happily accepted they were an item and that they were eager to have their share of our visit.

Susanne always had been a very sporty person and for a while trained as an ice skater with a club that produced more than one World and Olympic champion. After her first successes she was approached with the suggestion that she should change to a special school where sport was the main subject and where the champions of the future were produced.

After careful consideration Susanne decided that she was not ready to submit her whole life to sport and so she declined. As sport was one of the means by which the DDR achieved worldwide appreciation, to refuse to do all one could for national pride was seen as a kind of treachery. She was banned from her club immediately. She was not even allowed to use the premises any longer and nobody cared what would happen to a highly trained person who stopped training so suddenly. Indeed, Susanne had some health problems afterwards but, considering all the doping scandals that came out later, it would probably have been far worse had she stayed with high-performance sport.

I had mentioned before that Susanne, in contrast to her mother, had been able to take her 'Abitur' due to her father's status as part of the working class. Now she studied at the University of Leipzig. Her talents lay with languages. She would have loved to read English and French, but that was not how it worked. You were allowed only one 'capitalist' language and had to study at least one 'socialist' language. She had chosen French and Russian. However, the only way she was allowed to study languages was in preparation to become a teacher. Very soon after it became possible she went to study at a French university for a year. She realised that she never really wanted to be a teacher and she changed to tourism. Besides French, she subsequently learned English, Spanish and Italian.

Her then fiancé was on the same teacher's training course. He came from Plauen, a town in the triangle between Saxony, Bavaria and the Czech Republic where his parents still lived. On a later occasion all of us went down to meet them. It was not far from the border and we took a stroll through the former no-man's land. The men suddenly raced up an abandoned watchtower and brought down some items of former equipment in a gesture of the triumph they felt at not being watched and kept behind barbed wires any longer. It was a wonderful childish gesture and I approved of it wholeheartedly.

On that first weekend there was a lot of laughter and happiness. But there were sombre moments as well. What hurt me most was that Ute and Eberhard had never been sent to a developing country. All these years by the promise of a different more exciting future they had been blackmailed and kept in limbo. All the time they had been urged to mount ever higher professional and social hurdles and they were under permanent observation as to whether they kept their pledges. As much as they had given up and worked hard, it had been to no avail. I would not even put it beyond the DDR authorities that from the very beginning the whole action had been nothing but a sham to enforce their submission.

And I had not been the only relative or friend with whom they had had to sever links. Ute had other relatives from her father's side who lived in West Berlin and West Germany. At the end of the day they and their friends had been forced to stay apart for... nothing! I for my part felt utterly cheated and I can't start to imagine what Ute and Eberhard must have felt when they eventually realised that they would never be allowed to go after all they had sacrificed.

22. Re-discovering the town

I was eager to go downtown and visit all the places I remembered. There is the mighty cathedral St. Mary and the St. Severin Church both on top of the cathedral hill with its wide staircase leading down to the enormous market place. (Both churches changed allegiance during the Reformation and became protestant for a while. Later they were returned to the Roman Catholic faith but, as the town's story goes, the great stairs stayed protestant and so the Catholics built their own private – and catholic - access at the back of the hill to reach their churches!)

Opposite the cathedral is Petersberg (Peter`s hill). This hill probably was already inhabited and used in prehistoric times. During Christianisation a monastery was built on top which grew and was reconstructed over the centuries. Very early on the place was used for Imperial Diets and subsequently was turned into a fort and later into a citadel. The military use of the place only ceased in 1964. Since then it is open to the public.

We visited the old town hall and the famous Kraemer Bridge, the one which has houses built on it. All the old land marks I remembered were there. But still I despaired at seeing the town so utterly run down. The dominant colour was grey; it seemed that hardly any house had seen a fresh coat of paint for the last twenty years. You could not imagine where to start the renovations for the town to become once more the historical jewel that it used to be. It seemed as if for many years the task of making the environment liveable and enjoyable had felt so overwhelming that most people and the town authorities had just given up on it.

The general attitude that everything was in vain anyway did not help. Not only the important historic sites were let down, you could see it in every street. Whatever would have helped to embellish the surroundings had been in notoriously short supply, might it be paint, bricks, slabs or plants. As a last resort people retreated into their own homes and there they concentrated whatever energies they had left to keep their private space inhabitable. The rest of the world was left to decay.

They say that you can kill a man with a house as well as with an axe. How could hope and the energy to change things emerge from such depressing surroundings? One of the reasons for a general listlessness, which was a permanent feature the secret Stasi reports deplored, was not difficult to detect.

Perhaps it is difficult to understand how heroic the day to day fight for supplies must have been when you live in a country where you just have to go to the shops to obtain nearly anything you could imagine. Before the 'Wende' whenever I visited Ute, I was always amazed to see lots of people, who, in the middle of the day you would have expected to be working. Often in overalls or other working clothes they had obviously interrupted their work to go chasing after their daily necessities. At any given time, half of the nation seemed to be out on a very stressful shopping trip and you wondered who meanwhile was fulfilling the production-plans.

How emotionally draining these permanent shortages must have been, we learnt, when Ute, Eberhard and the young couple soon returned our visit. A dated law still existed then from the time when only a handful of East Germans could travel to West Germany. It stated that every individual should get a present of 100, - DM, taking into account that visitors from the DDR would have only small or no currency allowance from their government. So, Ute's family now possessed 400, - DM, which seemed like a small fortune to them.

Of course, they wanted to make the most of it. Michael took Eberhard to a DIY shop to help him choose a few tools and appliances for their house in Erfurt. Michael told me afterwards - and he was visibly moved - that Eberhard started to cry in front of all the shelves of nails and screws, electrical goods, wallpapers and tins of paint. Those were the tears, Michael told me, of someone who was utterly exhausted by all the tricks and treats he had to play to get what he needed, and suddenly found himself being drowned by all the riches he had ever dreamed of. The two men left in a hurry as Eberhard could not take it any longer. And he was not the only one. There were different reactions to what must have been a deep cultural shock but at the end of the day each of our visitors admitted to being totally shattered.

The access to material goods was only one aspect of the changes the former DDR citizens faced and probably the least important, although the first reaction, of course, was to go for all those things they been denied for such a long time. However, I was very keen to see how the sudden freedom of expression, the feeling of not being watched any longer and the open borders would touch people's hearts.

The historical event was very soon baptised 'die Wende', (the turnaround). This choice of word indicates the difficulty in finding a correct expression for a unique experience. The German 'Wende' hints at something close to destiny, something that was set in motion by forces beyond any individual or collective power. The term has little connotation of actions taken. The much more active "revolution" was hardly ever used, although the people themselves brought the changes about. However, there had never been a master plan, no program to overthrow the old system and establish a new one. There had been no army marching, no machinegun-fire in the cobbled streets of the old town centre. No radio station had been taken by storm, although the imposing buildings of the Stasi had been occupied before the majority of documents could have been destroyed by those who had inflicted so much pain while collecting them. There was no particular moment when the balance shifted in a single dramatic act. It was more as though the weight of all those sorrows that had accumulated over such a long time had burdened down the system to breaking point. A feeling of inevitability was shared widely so that even those in power made hardly any move to stop the avalanche. Step by step things progressed and changed while the old government remained with all their means of control. But suddenly all those 'power tools' seemed utterly blunt. On a lighter note, one could say that people had suddenly realised that the emperor's new clothes had hardly ever covered his ugly body. Repression always has two sides: those who threaten people and those who submit readily to the slightest threat out of fear not of what really happens but of what *might* happen to them. Now the population had taken the decision that 'enough was enough', and that they would not be forced into submission any longer.

At first tens of thousands of demonstrators chanted: "We are the People!", until it was obvious that nobody would dare to deny them the right to decide their own future. Free and secret general elections took place and a new government was established in the DDR. Then, however, the agenda changed. While politicians and "Round Tables" were still fighting over a new constitution for the DDR and the future relationship between the Federal Republic and the Democratic Republic, people on the street in East Germany changed their chant to: "We are ONE people!" thus conspicuously indicating what they really wanted.

Still people did not trust their own power and found it hard to believe that they themselves had provoked the historical changes. Therefore, the word which entered the vernacular, whenever one wanted to indicate the "before" and "after", was "die Wende", although to my strongest belief many could be utterly proud of the part they had played in the first successful and peaceful revolution on German soil.

All my life I have longed to experience that overwhelming feeling which I thought would erupt when people realised they were suddenly liberated from oppression. I remember my parents recounting what a relief they felt when the war ended. How full of hope the eventual downfall of the Nazis was for them in spite of all the hardship and difficulties in the years to come. With all their hearts they had flung themselves into everything that had previously been forbidden like jazz music, international literature, modern art, drama and cinema. After the war the situation in the bombed cities must have been desperate but somehow, they improvised and greedily savoured every morsel of culture they could lay their hands on.

I love the tale about those small theatres where as a rule you did not only pay the price for a ticket but you had to bring pieces of coal in order to have the room warm enough to play in. While chairs were in short supply, they used tables, pianos and whatever else could serve as seats. My parents' favourite place actually was on the piano, as from there they had the best view.

Although we three lived in only one room, my

parents held the most swinging of parties there. On one occasion the whole room was decorated like a pirate ship and the drinks were kept cold in my baby bath tub. The only ball gown my mother had was made from leftovers of parachute silk, sewn by hand with a major input by my father who could do really, really minute stitches.

I myself did get a glimpse of this kind of euphoria on different occasions. I told you about my time in Prague in 1968, when people realised that their opposition made such a difference. Years later I joined in for a summer after the revolution of 1974 in Portugal. For a few weeks we worked on a big real estate in the Alentejo area. The manager, who had represented the absentee landlord in a rather horrid way, had been chased away by the landless farm labourers who now tried to turn the rundown place into a profitable enterprise in common ownership. Those labourers who had always lived in utter poverty were in their overwhelming majority illiterate and for them medical care was virtually non-existing. We helped them to drill wells and to get electricity to the main farm buildings which were turned into a school and a clinic. The whole atmosphere then was electrifying because everything seemed possible and people fought for what they believed in with all their might.

I expected my East German friends would feel a similar kind of elation because a door to the world had suddenly opened and painful political and social pressures had ceased. But it did not happen that way or at least it did not happen suddenly.

Of course, there were the first few days when everybody in East or West Germany ran around shouting: "This is unbelievable!" Friends of ours spontaneously bought kilos of bananas (!) and put bunches of them on every parked car which displayed an East German number plate. They thought it would make more sense than to put flowers behind the windscreen-wipers as many other people did. To decorate those cars whose owners were probably strolling around in a West German town for the first time in their lives was only one of a multitude of gestures ordinary people performed all over Germany to express their profound happiness.

But after the first joy had ceased, in the East it gave way to a funny mixture of life going on very much as usual and a rather anxious anticipation about what would happen next. Obviously if you had always been told what to do and what to think to be suddenly left alone was not only positive. It did make you feel deeply insecure as well. Ute explained it to me once when she said: "We expected that the ruling culture would be replaced by another ruling culture which would be similar exclusive. When we understood that suddenly each of us had to find our own individual way through a maze of possibilities, it was like stepping into a void. More than anything else it was frightening."

23. The General Line

There is one example of what I would like you to understand. It has nothing to do with Ute and her experiences but it was very typical. For me it was an eye opener. As I told you before, at that time I was employed by an institution that operated nationwide and offered vocational training to adults, especially to the unemployed. There was a huge demand for retraining courses in the former DDR so we expanded into the East quite quickly taking on board lots of new colleagues locally.

At my level of responsibility, we had regular nation-wide meetings in order to exchange experiences and to help each other with examples of best practices. I became friends with one of our new managers from Chemnitz (which was still called Karl-Marx-Stadt then). He was a wonderful creative and humorous guy and we all liked him very much. We really thought we had welcomed him with open arms so we were utterly shocked when one night after the official meeting was over and we all relaxed over a pint of beer, he suddenly attacked us quite furiously. He blamed us for 'not allowing him in'. We had no idea what he was talking about and for a while the argument seemed utterly aimless as if we spoke different languages. It took us half the night to work out what went wrong between us. At the heart of this outburst of frustration was his lifelong experience that there was always a 'general line', set by the Party. Everybody was aware of it and as long as one towed the line, one at least avoided conflicts. With us this man now found himself with a group of twenty or more people who were as different as people could be. He overheard our heated discussions and noted that often we could not agree and left it at that. And yet we all worked within the same company and within the same system of vocational education. Therefore, he was convinced there had to be a hidden 'general line', and if he could not find out what it was, it was because we denied him this essential information. Thus, he felt threatened as a person and in his position. It came to him as a shock and I do not know whether he really believed us when we tried to convince him that such a general line simply did not exist. We were organised in what economists call 'profit centres' and the truth was: it was each man/woman for him/herself. The remarkable thing about this episode was that on both sides of the argument it had taken us so long to understand what the problem was because wherever we came from we thought that those basic truth were self-evident. He never thought he had to explain about 'general lines'. We were convinced everybody understood that our success was measured only by how many courses we would be able to sell in a highly competitive but locally diversified market. Which party we voted for, which beliefs we held individually, which attitude we had towards the teaching of adults, had little to do with it.

Some premises are so deeply ingrained into your

political or social culture that you have to be confronted by a totally alien world of ideas to realise that there *could* be other approaches to reality. That was and is true for the situation in Germany and probably for all scenes where fundamentally different cultures meet. I believe that this is one of the main reasons why tensions remained between East and West Germans. The societies we grew up in were so different and while hurrying to re-unite and to put the infra-structure in place we forgot to take the time to go back to the basics and start a proper exchange concerning those deeply held beliefs and attitudes.

One of the ways this tension between East and West manifested itself was in nicknames. There were the 'Wessis' (West), the opposite then logically being 'Ossie' (Ost = East). The Ossies thought the Wessis to be loud and arrogant. One of the reasons being because Wessis had been aware for a very long time of their rights as citizens and customers and acted accordingly by demanding adequate services, while Ossis still experienced themselves as petitioners for scarce goods. And professionally while they had been taught never to stick out in a crowd Wessis knew that when you wanted to climb up the career ladder you had to be self-assured and you sometimes had to use your elbows.

'Behaving like a 'Wessie'' became a running gag between Ute and myself. I remember the day when Ute told me that she had 'done a Wessi'. She had felt badly treated by her local bank and had gone to the manager to complain. Telling me about it, she sounded amused, proud and yet a bit ashamed. Today, as her daughter Susanne has been living and working in West Germany for many years, Ute still sometimes remarks that Susanne has become a real Wessi. Sometimes that is meant as a compliment – sometimes not.

But how could she or others have learnt to behave like confident citizens or customers, when they had almost always been treated as the subjects of a power wielded by an ever-present but anonymous party, and as far as consumption was concerned, most of the time all they could do was to take their place demurely in lengthy queues? Convincing staff to be nice or polite to customers was not part of any professional training, it seemed. The customer was far from being king there. Likewise, the representative of the state had every interest to intimidate and not to flatter their citizens.

Foremost the newly gained freedom was understood as freedom to consume. Thus, the seemingly unlimited provision of material goods was appreciated quite quickly. But still demand was limited to a few goods, which I found quite fascinating. Obviously, you only wish for things which represent a certain value to you. Most of the former DDR citizens had been watching West TV for most of their lives and thus had been confronted with advertisements and lifestyle alternatives. However, as all those goods had been so totally out of reach, the achievable "keeping up with the Joneses" played a major role in decisions what was desirable and what was not. The neighbours bought a Skoda which was far more desirable than a Trabant? You shared their opinion having lived within the same supply system and went for a Skoda as well. That you could go for a Mercedes Benz or a BMW was considered absolutely over the top and only for impostors who pretended to be Wessis which was despicable.

If you thought about buying a new living room cabinet you would like one similar to the one which had just been delivered to the neighbours' house. It was desirable because you knew it had been ordered a long time ago and the neighbours were lucky to eventually having got one. Unusual or designed furniture was not even considered to be worth looking at. It was not beautiful, it was just strange. Nobody they knew furnished his living room like that and so nobody felt the worse for not doing it.

Open borders meant that people could travel. A whole new world was calling. Did they travel? In a manner of speaking they did. Coach tours were all the rage. To see Paris, Vienna, Venice, if only for a few days, fulfilled what had always seemed a mad dream. At the beginning there was a kind of rush, as nobody was sure what the future would bring. The gap in the Wall might close again any day. However, those trips not only had to be cheap, they had to be *guided* tours. And no Wessis on the coach, please! It was much safer to stick to your own kind and to load the responsibility for the nitty-gritty upon the shoulders of a professional guide, who would keep everyone under control.

Of course, that had to do with their earlier experiences. East Germans had been allowed to travel within the eastern bloc, but in those countries, they had found the same kind of restrictions and rationing as at home. Occasionally, when they shared holiday resorts with Western visitors, as in Bulgaria, they were painfully aware that they were only second-class tourists, due to their lack of hard currency.

Whether at home or abroad holiday places had to be applied for and it was through the trade union's representative at work that one was allocated to a holiday resort. There one would be surrounded by other members of the collective, housed in rather limited accommodation under a fairly strict regime. It was one room per family, so whatever age the children were, they had to share the room with their parents. The meals had to be taken at a specific time in a kind of canteen, with the next group of people already queuing for your table. If you did not want to fit yourself into this routine all you could do was either to go camping if you were lucky enough to get some space on the few camping grounds or to seek for private accommodations, which were rare and did cost a fortune. If you had to supply yourself the daily struggle for necessities would be even more difficult than at home, as you did not know the turf and could not make special relationships work. Ute told me that on nearly every occasion when they were eventually allowed a holiday on the Baltic Sea, they returned home early as they found the holidays extremely stressful.

Michael's relatives after the "Wende" bought their 'Datscha' (Russian expression for summerhouse) from their former employer. As holiday places were so rare often firms had improvised their own provisions which then were reserved only for their own employees. Today the building is a wooden chalet with most modern amenities but it started as a kind of garden shed. It is still rather small, but how much more cramped it must have been before the lounge and a proper bathroom had been added! While it was under the management of the factory two families had one bedroom each and had to share a kitchenette and a toilet; all that in a mountainous area with a rough climate where you could end up with days and weeks of rain and heavy snow in the winter. Still Michael's relatives were very fond of the place because of happy memories when they were allowed to holiday there.

Due to those experiences the encouragement that now East Germans could travel wherever they wished to with whatever means took their fancy, for as long as their money lasted, was at first met with blank stares.

24. Food for Thought

A lot of books were published in the DDR, but of course they only reflected the official ideology. Authors who strayed from the party line very quickly found themselves under pressure. Some managed to smuggle their manuscripts out for publication in West Germany. The DDR took the hard currency that was earned abroad, thank you very much, but that did not mean those writers were allowed to enjoy the fruits of their international fame. As much as the DDR tried to retain its citizens, many members of the artistic world, writers, musicians, actors etc. were eventually allowed to or were forced to emigrate just because those in power preferred to be rid of them.

Now people could read whatever they wanted. Yes, but where to start? For many people literature had meant the same socialist catch words, the prescribed optimistic morals chewed over again and again. It was so boring! Even educated and well-read people like Ute took a bit of time to discover that there was a whole world of literature which previously they had been prevented from exploring. While Ute and Eberhard had been preparing for a French speaking African country they had started to learn French and had studied some chosen French authors. This was *the* French literature, they believed, as they were accustomed to certain limitations in subject and style in their own literature. To have been confronted with the width and depth of the rest of

French or any other literature was an eye opener.

Philosophy and history were important subjects in DDR-education. They were the basis of a socialist society. But there was only one kind of philosophy, dialectic materialism, and history was interpreted according to those ideas. So, by the third or fourth time that the same subject in the same way was presented at school or at college people were so fed up by what they felt were only slogans that they just stopped listening. They had always been told that this was all that was worth knowing. After they understood 'dialectic materialism' there was no more to philosophise about.

One Christmas I tried to find a suitable present for Ute. It occurred to me that Michael and I very much enjoyed reading a monthly magazine on history. So, I presented Ute with a gift subscription for a year. Ute loved it and when the year was over she continued with the subscription. As we regularly talk about what we have read Ute often states how much she still feels cheated. "There is so much more than we were taught. And even things we knew about have so many more aspects than I was ever told."

How to approach political controversy was also difficult. When you are not accustomed to public discussion, other than by repeating the party line in not so many words, how can you be appreciative when you are confronted with different and even irreconcilable opinions and there is no one to tell you what is right or what is wrong in the end?

In East Germany they had lived for so long with

the strong suspicion that they were being told lies by their authorities. Remarkably enough this did not lead to a cynical view of the future. People hoped that now, whit everything changing - and hopefully changing for the better - the representatives of this new and different system would eventually speak the truth (and that there was only one truth!). They did not want to hear about different aspects, opinions and diverse standpoints with no clue as to which one was the right one. Thus, in the beginning there was a tendency to believe the new politicians more than they deserved - and more than hardened and slightly cynical citizens of established democracies ever would have done. Equally strong was the disappointment when at the end of the day elected politicians could not keep their promises. Somehow a strong belief was still prevalent that those in power could perform miracles if only they wanted to. If things did not go the way the public wanted, it had to be because those in power maliciously held back. Subsequently at the next election those politicians were punished by a hefty swing towards the former opposition. Thus, they gave each political orientation a try and became more and more disillusioned because things did not change fast enough. That social and economic change depends on more than the goodwill of an elected government still seems the most alien of all political concepts for many people.

The sad and dangerous thing is that some start to blame democracy in general for all they miss, such as many Germans did during the 'Weimar' time, and that a certain longing for a "strong" leader or government is raising its ugly head. Neo-Nazis with all their chauvinistic brutality and their racism have some support where no one else seems to care.

Equally, nostalgia paints the past brighter than it ever was. There are areas in the former DDR where any party in succession of the SED would find a strong support and party representatives would no longer make any attempt to hide the fact that in their former lives they served the Stasi faithfully.

The attitude to expect the truth and nothing but the truth transferred to most other means of public communications, including advertisements. The products which now flooded into the East brought their Western style of public relations with them – and in many cases it did not work. People in East Germany expected understandable information on a product. The propagation of a certain life-style by creating an atmosphere without really dealing with the product did not catch their imagination. There had been only one life-style. There had been no choice. What could be desirable about choices if basically products and prices were the same and only the name and the wrapping changed? Choice for the sake of choice was not necessarily seen as a virtue.

In the first years, however, there was a prevalent aversion against their own well-known products, those in whose production they even might have been engaged themselves. There was no trust what-so-ever in the quality of home-grown products. Western products had to be better whatever they were. For the West German industry this brought a huge boost while that in the East collapsed even more quickly than it would have been necessary. Of course, there were lines of productions which were totally out of date and destructive for men and the environment, but others could have survived if only there would have been a market for the goods.

Meanwhile the wave of nostalgia comprises not only ideas and memorabilia but typical DDR products as well. A lot of those, especially groceries, beer and other spirits, have found their way to the markets under their old name and often they are excellent. Now they find customers all over Germany, as for West Germans they offer new tastes of a part of the country which was unknown to them before.

25. What remains

During all the years since the 'Wende' Ute has helped me to understand what was going on. Emotionally we were always so close that I was able to witness history developing through her eyes. For me it was and still is a moving experience.

On the other hand, Michael and I were glad that we were able to help out with practical advice about how "our" systems such as social security, health and unemployment insurance work and how to choose the right kind of bank services. We were able to warn them to avoid those fraudulent offers that swept East Germany. Thus, we assisted them in a lot of unavoidable decisions they had to take in this brave new world. Meanwhile we have established a sisterly telephone routine and we continue to visit each other regularly.

In 1992 on one of our visits to Erfurt we landed in the middle of a festival. It was the celebration of the 1250th anniversary of the first document mentioning of Erfurt in the year 742. One of the highlights was a long and colourful pageant winding through the centre of town. It was a wonderful sunny day and at least half of Erfurt's population attended. In the town's tight budget there was no money for such frivolities and private enterprises as potential sponsors had only just started. Thus, most of that pageant was creatively improvised by individuals or groups of volunteers who used whatever they could lay their hands on.

Some tableaux might have lacked historical correctness because the proper kind of costumes or decorations was not available. However, amongst all the fun and laughter that did not matter at all. For costumes the theatre's stores kindly had opened their doors and had been plundered. Obviously, it was not easy to find the right person to fit into the given sizes and shapes of the clothes. The search had not always been successful with hilarious results. Damsels in distress marched in flowing robes and bulky trainers, kings wore theatrical crowns as a sign of their royal might and a famous archbishop looking very much like Santa Claus.

While the procession moved through the town centre, one or other of the knights lost his pride and his helmet. It was really very, very hot and to move around in full armour must have been torture. Costumed riders on horses and on the odd - more or less well behaved - donkey moved down the streets. For the floats, local farmers had brought their tractors and trailers into town and most of them displayed Erfurt's famous flowers. There were many private cars decorated in aspects of Erfurt's history, as well as wheelbarrows, prams and anything else that would move on wheels. It was wonderfully colourful and good-humoured. There was food, beer and wine from stalls and a splendid time was had by all.

Somewhere en route we had lost sight of Ute and Eberhard and when we caught up with them we discovered that Ute was crying. We were quite shocked and asked anxiously what was wrong. She told us that nothing was wrong, but that suddenly, while she was feeling extremely cheerful, she remembered that all these participants and spectators were present because they *wanted* to be there. Nobody had ordered them to come out and wave flags or applaud. They had *volunteered* to take part. Everyone was *happy* to be here. And realising this she had started to cry.

For many years you could still wind her up on the First of May by asking why she was not taking part in the traditional demonstration, as was her duty. She always would start to defend herself, until she would realise you were only pulling her leg, and then she would give you an earful about what it really meant to be ordered to join an equally desinterested crowd in the early hours of a cold morning. People had had to gather hours before the procession started, had had to stand in line and wait and wait until eventually it was their turn to march past the local establishment, shouting their undying support and waving their flags.

What life in the DDR really had been like and what has changed often surfaces in those little anecdotes. On one occasion Ute heaved a deep sigh over a full-grown hangover after a late night with friends.

"But at least" she said," these days I can get drunk without being afraid."

Why was she afraid to get drunk? I asked, thinking she was referring to a health problem.

"No, she said, it was only that during all these years I did not trust myself. I might have said something which could have been held against me. Therefore, I never really joined in. I always tried to stay sober."

Sometimes one can hear people say with a certain kind of nostalgia that in the old DDR personal relationships were so much better and that there was a general feeling of solidarity while nowadays everybody only cares for himself. I beg to differ. Undoubtedly due to shortages in so many fields, there always was a strong necessity to network. How one obtained daily necessities or the few luxuries that were not totally out of reach, and who knew whom with special contacts, gave topics for hours and hours of conversation and for many jokes. Once the urgent need for these communications vanished, it easily happened that people suddenly realised that, beyond the solving of practical problems, they really had not all that much in common.

With the possibility of expressing themselves about everything freely they might have found out that they really did not share many political, social or philosophical attitudes with those they had thought of as allies before. There had been many things you just did not discuss, and even if you did, most people found it safer to follow the party line. Nobody would dare to contradict openly what had been postulated by the Party. Now often arguments erupted where before there had ruled a false sense of harmony.

One of the basics of life in the DDR was a strong

demand that the most desirable way of living was to be like the next person and that ambitions, if they existed at all, had to be altruistic. Now it became obvious how much some people wanted to better their lives, while others still insisted that society should mainly care for them and their needs. Both groups soon developed a health disdain for the opposition and a split opened wider and wider between the winners and the losers of the re-unification process.

Therefore, in many personal relationships the dice was thrown anew, some friendships survived and deepened, others did not. What vanished was the necessity to shut up and scratch each other's back. And to tell you the truth: I am not sure whether that is not rather a relief than a loss.

On a more sinister note for many people the possibility to take a look into their Stasi dossier destroyed personal relationships profoundly. They suffered the unbelievable pain at finding out that their nearest and dearest had informed on them, thus often hindering their career or bringing other troubles upon them.

The opening of the Stasi archives ended more than one promising career or at least shed a shadow over the reputation of the person in question. Some imposing public figures were found out to have been informal Stasi informants. Many of the new members of the first and last freely elected DDR parliament eventually had to admit to their murky past and subsequently lost voters' support as quickly as they had gained it.

There is no denying that there are people who feel that with the end of the DDR they have lost out. It was enlightening to learn what those people considered to be their main loss. Some of Michael's relatives yielded a certain kind of power through work-related positions which made it advisable for their colleagues not to fall out with them. They still bemoan the end of the former order, although they would readily admit to the fact that in many ways they are better off now. It taught me that to be well off can be utterly relative. Before, they did not have that much but they had more than the rest, and people considered them to be special. Now everybody was better off and there was nothing special about them anymore. As Michael's cousin exclaimed on one occasion:

"After all, we had everything we needed and we had friends in places to fix things for us if it was necessary!"

After the "Wende" they and their friends lost whatever little power they ever had and that was difficult to digest.

Of course, there were *real* losses and they were considerable, the most important being the loss of absolute security of employment. Before the re-unification and the opening of the economy unemployment was virtually unknown in the DDR. Even people who would not be able to hold down a job at all were always kept on board. The sad fact is that the DDR paid a high price for this with a terribly low rate of productivity. Together with politically controlled prices, which were unreasonably low, it led to a substantial lack of funding for all kinds of improvements in production, protection of the environment and developments in infrastructure.

The fact that you would not be made redundant whatever happened, of course had an impact on the mental attitude towards work and the effort the individual would put into it. The ever-present lack of materials, the necessity to chase everyday supplies, the social pressure to conform and the described job security had the effect that many people had no reason to over-engage in what they were doing.

There are a thousand and one stories of what happened when, after the "Wende", different work ethics clashed brutally. The owner of a small company in our area in West Germany which produces machinery told me what happened when he employed an East German worker shortly after it became possible to do so. On the first morning this man accidentally broke his main tool. He put it down and prepared to leave his workplace. When asked what he thought he was doing the man answered that, now that his tool was broken, there was nothing else for him to do and therefore he was going home. His foreman opened a cupboard, showed him a store with a hundred similar tools and told him that he could only go home before the end of his shift if all those were broken as well. His new employee was neither stupid nor lazy, he only reacted how he had always reacted and it had made sense under his former circumstances. He could not imagine that there would be a never-ending stream of supplies and a thing like "Just-in-time-production" was beyond his horizon.

Privatising across the whole range of industry in East Germany meant that certain sectors such as chemical plants and open cast coal mines were closed down as the installations were antiquated and run down beyond repair. Also, the impact on the environment and on people's health was so terrible that closure was the only sensible thing to do. Some factories were closed because, due to their low productivity, they were unable to compete on the now open markets. Others were bought by national and international competitors only to be closed quickly to clean up the market.

A lot of tax payer's money was used to try and kick-start the economy. Admittedly quite a lot was wasted or disappeared into dark channels. In the beginning there was a gold-digging atmosphere. Investors and Entrepreneurs looked for the fast buck with more or less sound business plans and there was little supervision to stop them doing so. The "Green Landscapes", the former Chancellor Kohl promised our new compatriots takes time to develop and, in a way, on both sides of the divide we still are waiting.

Meanwhile the economic situation in East Germany has widely diversified. Although unemployment is still higher than in West Germany (and it is not low in West Germany either) some areas and people in the former DDR are doing quite well. Unfortunately, in other areas, things are simply desperate and people have moved away in droves to find employment elsewhere.

There are different reasons for this slow progress. Of course, one is the influence of globalisation, when jobs, especially in the industrial sector, tend to go to countries where labour is cheaper. With countries like Poland and the Czech Republic as neighbours fierce competition is right on the door step. On the other hand, consumer's demand for services remains more limited than in other comparable countries as people have yet to get accustomed to buying that which they had previously organised themselves. Furthermore, in an insecure situation, when your job may be on the line, you would think twice about spending money on things which you would not consider essential.

People have been told that they all are citizens of one country now and of course they desire to reach the same level of income as in other parts of Germany as soon as possible. Individually they have every right to compare their efforts to those of West German employees. However, while productivity there still remains lower than in other industrial countries, this demand collectively is difficult to fulfil and diminishes the chances for new investment which would be necessary to widen the basis of employment.

A certain lack of personal initiative should be no surprise as any initiative at all had been suppressed for such a long time. Of course, after losing their former governmentally controlled and guaranteed jobs and with little chance to find other employment, some people have become self-employed, some very successfully, others doing not so well. However, many people would still hope for (or dream of) the one huge factory that would provide jobs for a whole town as it used to be before. So instead of becoming active themselves they would rather sit at home, collect their un-employment money and wait for the day when they would be called up to take their place on a production-line without too many questions being asked.

But those times are over. Unfortunately for any development the more mobile and creative people tend to leave East Germany and move to West Germany. Thus, the population of East Germany is and has been declining for some time. Those who stay behind often are pensioners enjoying a level of pension much higher that what they would have had to expect from their former state, or the less mobile, less well educated which leads to all kind of social problems. Thus, right-wing ideas, Nazism and racism unfortunately find a more fertile ground there as one would have expected after forty years of anti-fascistic education.

With the decline of population some of the newly built infra-structure or the beautifully restored town centres now are oversized and seem eerily void of users. Towns have started to build back housings estates, especially those standardised pre-fabricated blocks of flats of which people used to be so proud. Now too many of those flats stand empty and are in danger of developing into slums. Areas which formerly had been developed now are turned again into open spaces, often parks and recreational grounds.

Ute's home town Erfurt, now the proud capital of the state of Thuringia, belongs to those parts that have improved tremendously and one can see it all over the place. Whenever Michael and I visit we take the same route around the inner city to see what is going on and what is new. In the beginning only the odd house had been restored and stood out of the mass of greyish derelicts. Now it is reversed. Most of the historical sites are in good condition and re-privatisation and grants have helped to embellish residential areas to the point that now Ute shakes her head disapprovingly over the few that are not yet reconstructed.

Private trade, supermarkets and boutiques have opened, along with department stores, book shops, art galleries, hotels, coffee houses, restaurants, discotheques and all that you would expect of a cultural and political centre. New railway tracks for faster trains and the enlarged and modernised airport now connect Erfurt to the rest of Germany and to the world.

Of Erfurt's pride, the old and famous university, only a few walls have survived. When it was founded in 1392 it was only the third in the German speaking realm. One of its famous students was Martin Luther. Unfortunately, after two waves of the plague in the 16th century, the university had gone into a long and slow decline and had eventually been closed in 1816.

However, Erfurt always was a place for higher education. After the Second World War it maintained colleges for medicine and for teacher training. For a long time, there were plans to bring those colleges together and make a new start with other subjects to re-constitute the traditional university. In 1994 this plan came true. The university was re-founded and meanwhile one faculty after the other has been established. By the way: English is the second language at this university, lectures and exams can be taken in English as well as in German.

With a lot of reconstruction being done very sensibly with due respect to the historical examples people of Erfurt can be really proud of their town. Ute's husband Eberhard through his craft was involved in some of the restorations. He regularly takes us around to point out where his firm has replaced old and derelict iron gates with perfect copies of historical originals. Nevertheless, he was the one person in the family to be threatened by unemployment because although there were enough commissions for the workshop which employed him, payment was slow (unfortunately even more so, when orders by the public services were involved). He eventually had to leave because his salary had not been paid for many months. It was a difficult time for him. He was a master locksmith and an excellent one as such and he knew that his craft remained in high demand. Still he found it difficult to find a new employer that could pay him an adequate wage for his age and experience.

In contrast to her husband's Ute's professional situation improved after the "Wende". She had been a deputy head for many years. Now she became headmaster of a primary school and had to guide her school through the fundamental changes that happened after the re-unification, when responsibility for education fell into the hand of Thuringia as part of the organisation of the Federal Republic.

There was hardly one stone left unturned and teachers and pupils alike had to follow a steep learning curve. Not only had nearly all textbooks to be replaced, but the whole atmosphere in daily school life changed. Before the 'Wende' pre-military education had had the above-mentioned important place in the education system, with rituals such as formal greetings and the shouting of slogans. That kind of discipline was not welcome any longer – although some still might wish it back.

For many parents, the fact that they were handed back the first responsibility for bringing up their children was a huge challenge. In a way the support system in the DDR encouraged people to have many children, because the more children they had, the more privileges they could claim. Furthermore, they were relieved of some in-built troubles of child-rearing because after the first few weeks the state would take over and would care for the children from morning to night. Many parents now found it extremely difficult to cope. They still expected the schools or other social services to fulfil their old roles of total caretakers. Ute is sometimes shocked by the extent to which parents still deny that it should be their job to care for or even feed their children and to teach them basic behavioural and other skills.

With the end of state-run total childcare and all the other uncertainties of life which confronted the former DDR citizens the birth rate in the area of the former DDR dropped dramatically. Quite sensibly many people wanted to wait until they had a clearer picture of their future before deciding to have children. Sometimes it turned out that one or both ended in long term unemployment and the financial strain did nothing to encourage them to have more children. Thus, the subsequent drop in numbers of children entering school meant that the re-organisation of schools became necessary.

The plan, when it was finally published, indicated that Ute's pupils would be merged with those of another primary school and the buildings would be taken over by a secondary school. For a year Ute was in a terrible limbo not knowing what would happen to her. By that time, she was a civil servant and as such she could not be made redundant. But this status implied that the ministry could send her wherever they wished and allocate her to any job they thought her fit to do. It was an anxious time for her, as understandably there were fewer positions for headmasters available than former headmasters waiting for a new assignment.

However, Ute was the only one to be anxious about her chances in the competition with other candidates for the remaining positions. Everybody else knew that she was excellently placed. She had done such a good job and had undertaken so many extra-activities to improve her school. And the authorities knew this too. Consequently, she was entrusted with another and even larger primary school, where she launched into the same effort to bring up standards and to improve the results.

There is a tragic footnote to Ute's professional success story. Close to her primary school stands a secondary school called "Johann Gutenberg Gymnasium". Both schools worked closely together. Most of Ute's pupils who after the first four years changed to a 'Gymnasium' would change to this school and Ute had lots of contacts with its teachers and administrators.

On the 26th of April 2002 a former pupil, 19-year-old Robert Steinhäuser, entered the Gutenberg Gymnasium heavily armed. He went on a killing spree taking the lives of sixteen people, most of them teachers, and in the end, he took his own. It was a terrible shock for everybody in the teaching community, for the city of Erfurt and for the rest of Germany. Ute was acquainted with more than one of the victims and Ute's school was so close to the crime scene that they found themselves included in the police cordon.

To mourn their dead more than 100.000 Erfurters (out of a population of 300.000) gathered a week later on the large square in front of the imposing cathedral and St. Severin church in a moving service. When we telephoned later in the afternoon Ute could hardly speak because of the depth of her horror and grief.

Still it is quite typical for us to search out each other's presence if only via telephone if something good or bad happens to us. After my husband and my father Ute would probably be the next person I would call if I had something really important to tell.

On the outside we are still as different as we have always been. Ute has always been a lady and I never will be one. She is more cautious, I remain more adventurous. She likes the South, France and Italy, the warmer the climate the better it is for her. I made a second home in Scotland and there I brave the midges in summer and the gales and the long dark nights in winter. Equally we do have our distinct differences in political and other attitudes. Ute held on to her protestant belief and now besides German and Mathematic teaches Religious Education in school. I have always been a happy heathen and see no reason to believe differently.

But perhaps due to the genes we share or some mysterious bond we find it easy to communicate. I can tell Ute things I would scarcely mention to anyone else for fear of sounding ridiculous. With her I know that she will not laugh nor think me rather weird. In the majority of cases she answers that this is exactly how she feels or reacts or dreams. And it works in both ways. I am touched by the way she expresses her deepest thoughts and I could not do it better. Very often we do similar things at the same time without knowing about it or we start to talk about the same thing at the same time. Now that we have both crossed the threshold into our years of maturity I am sure that we will grow old together and be as close as this as long as we live.

26. What happened afterwards

You could call this an epilogue, but instead of a conciliatory summary it is just a new chapter about what happened to us in the meantime and what happened in Germany.

Many years have passed, since I wrote down Ute's and my story. Then I did it, because British friends asked me to do so. They felt that our story reflected the history of Germany after WW II in a remarkable way. Although our experiences would not have been unusual for many German families, there were a lot of aspects, especially of the everyday-life of ordinary people, of which they, the British, had only little idea. And I am afraid to say that this might not have changed a bit in the years inbetween.

When I read through what I had written down all then, I found no reason to change it profoundly, nothing, where I had been totally wrong or where my feelings and predictions had led me totally astray.

But of course, history and our personal stories proceed all the time. The perhaps subconscious hope that after the end of the 'Cold War', we would enter an age of peace and harmony was as wrong as every other hope people ever had in the progress of human history.

In 2021 Germany witnessed the end of the era of Chancellor Angela Merkel. She was not only the first female Chancellor of the BRD, but the first head of government, who had grown up and lived in the former GDR. From 2005 to 2021 she led the German government and the country through more than one crisis and even I, still being a 'Green', who had never voted for her, did not dislike her as a person and supported a lot of her decisions.

Furthermore, from 2012 to 2017 Joachim Gauck held the office of German President. He was one of those protestants actively in opposition to the GDR system and for ten years after the end of this regime (from 1990 to 2000) he was the head of the agency which took possession of and dealt with the Stasi files. He was the first President not to be affiliated to a specific political party, but being chosen with big public support for his life's work.

So, for some years the two most important offices of the Federal Republic were held by people who had grown up, lived and worked in the former GDR. There still might be positions of power and influence which people from the former GDR think are harder for them to reach, but all in all I believe that sooner or later this won't be a problem any longer.

The German reunification or the accession of the former GDR to the Federal Republic of Germany was an enormous joint undertaking. Just to give you a number: up to now it costs about 2 trillion Euros. Most of those costs occurred within the social-system-transfers, money transferred for pensions, benefits of all kind, re-training and un-employment-support. The rest was and is investments in infrastructure and support for companies.

After a time of economic hardship with high

numbers of unemployment in most parts of the country, but especially in the former GDR, Germany meanwhile has reached a quite satisfying economical position, depending strongly on industry and export. But still the situation in the east is not totally equal to that in the west. The reasons have been manifold and some have been implied before.

One reason might be that a whole generation of active and mobile people quickly moved to the west to find employment there. While people move to jobs, jobs do not move to people in the same speed.

Ute's daughter Susanne is one of those who moved. After finishing her studies in tourism in Heidelberg, she has been living and working not far from my old hometown Frankfurt/Main for many years now and travelled the whole world.

When we talk about economic success and rates of employment, it is obvious now that the area of the former GDR splits into parts which are quite prosperous, like the capitals of the individual Bundesländer and other cities, and other, mostly rural areas which are somehow left behind. But this is true of all parts of Germany: It makes a big difference whether you live in a metropolitan area or whether you find yourself far away from satisfying infra structures like public transport, internet access etc.

But what happens step by step is that many seemingly backward parts develop into tourist spots or places to retire to for the beauty of the countryside, the purity of nature, the nearness to the Baltic Coast or for the castles and houses of the former gentry, many of which have been turned into hotels and guesthouses.

While the specific economic problems of the German regions might be solvable in due course, increasingly there are more frightening ones which we seem to share with the rest of the world.

There seems to be a worldwide wave of anger and dissatisfaction which leads to people following right-wing populists who promise easy solutions for all their problems and offer the scarecrow of *an enemy* to whom people can attach all their frustrations. In that process reality and facts are the first victims. It is replaced by opinions without any proof of relevance, supported by absurd internet bubbles. And what is really horrible is that those conspiracy plots nearly always go hand in hand with scorn for democracy, praise for authoritarian leaders and all kinds of racist attitudes.

This is not a German phenomenon alone. There are enough example of the damage and hurt this inflicts all over the world.

But the wider trend plays out very specifically in those parts of Germany which used to be the old GDR, and remarkably even stronger, where during the GDR time people were unable to follow West German radio and television, i.e. Saxony.

In the beginning the malcontents in the former GDR often voted for 'Die Linke' ('The Left' – a party which developed out of the remains of the old SED) as a demonstration of their protest against the new political system. While the opposition was obviously directed against Capitalism, very often it included a deep-seated mistrust against Democracy, as it was understood and practised in the Federal Republic.

As a reaction to emigrants and refugees entering Germany (especially in 2015/16) these voters moved from the left to the right and much of the protest became openly violent and racists. Mainly in Saxony and in other areas of the former GDR, movements like Pegida (Patriotische Europäer gegen die Islamisierung des Abendlandes – Patriotic Europeans against the Islamization of the Occident) and the new right-wing party AFD (Alternative für Deutschland – Alternative for Germany) enjoy their greatest successes.

The party AFD was founded originally by people who disliked that the Euro should replace the Deutsch Mark. Those founders were socially conservative and economically liberal. But with the first success in elections it quickly became a reservoir for right-wingers, fascists and neo-Nazis of all provenances. The original founders have left long ago and today the AFD is openly racists, authoritarian and proclaims a future for Germany which could have come out of the Nazi propaganda in the thirties of the last century.

When I wrote the original text, I made you aware of the strength of the Neo-Nazi Party in parts of the former GDR. This party has all but vanished now and has been seamlessly replaced by the AFD.

Not surprising that in the same aerasahort Russia's Putin is still considered a hero and that for many of the former voters of 'Die Linke' the way to the right seems to be very short and easy.

Unfortunately, this is true even for some politicians of 'Die Linke', who try to regain their former support by political attitudes which are not all that different from those of the AFD. They end up in a trap of their own making: as the working masses must always be right and a socialist party should only be the mouthpiece for them, if those masses behave xenophobic or racist (or decline to be vaccinated against Covid) the Party has not only a duty to follow them, but to march in front.

Thus, perhaps 'Die Linke' – without really wanting it – is mimicking what happened in the Weimarer Republic, when Communists and Fascists sometimes worked together against the nascent democracy.

The main complaint of the malcontents in the former GDR seems to be that they feel short-changed. They feel they are not be respected enough and too much would be done for anybody else but them. They seem to long for a strong dictatorial leader and to hate the difficult and lengthy processes within a parliamentary democracy to bring any kind of change.

They will tell you that they want to be heard, but mean that they don't want anybody else to be heard as well. While demonstrating - even violently – without seriously being stopped by the legal forces, they pretend they are not allowed to express their opinions. Whoever is not of their opinion is called a liar or a traitor. All the media, of course, are liars, as long as they try to report halfway correctly or include all sides into their reporting.

Perhaps the experience to have been successful once with a quick and total change of system gives them the feeling they could do it again. Only this time in a totally different and dangerous direction.

Ute and I might not agree in every political aspect, but we both deeply abhor those developments. Again, Ute in Erfurt is closer to the problem as Thuringia is not free from these political movements.

She is retired now and is still living in the house that always was. But by now she lives there alone, as her beloved husband Eberhard died suddenly and much too soon some years ago. And her daughter Susanne leads her own life in another part of Germany.

For the first time in her life she now has reached a situation of maximum self-determination: living in her own house, being financially secure, no more duties either as daughter, wife, mother, boss or as colleague, she is just herself, can come and go how she pleases, follow her interests and avoid what she dislikes. She very bravely has taken the maintenance of her house into her own hands. And of course, she has faithful friends and neighbours who always are willing to lend a helping hand. So, all in all, although she misses her husband every day of her life, she enjoys and makes good use of her new independence.

Michael and I, after retiring, have returned to Bavaria. We now live in a small town not far from Munich, in the best of both worlds: the city is just a short train ride away and it takes us the same time to reach the Alpes or some wonderful lakes.

Since the beginning of 2020 the world has to deal with the Covid pandemic. The disease caught up with us while we were on a cruise around the world. Eventually we reached Europe and Germany again at the end of April 2020 and since then we live under changing restrictions, like the rest of the world.

The Germans often had a reputation of being especially obedient to authorities. In the reaction to the pandemic this turned out to be not really the case. Our vaccination rates are not overwhelming and there are lots of demonstrations – sometimes even violent ones – against those rules which are there to protect us against the pandemic. There was even a murder when a young man was shot because he demanded that a customer wears a mask.

There are two main groups of people who resist those necessary public rules, from denying that Covid exists at all to those who accept that it exists but don't want to wear a mask or to be vaccinated.

The first group are the same who would vote for parties like the AFD and they spread the same lies that other right-wing movements all around the world are spreading. Consequently, these Covid etc deniers are strong in Saxony and in other areas of the former GDR.

The other main group of those not wanting to be vaccinated are people with a special attitude towards health, alternative medicines and natural healing. Those ideas sometimes are shared by people who are not that far from our own political convictions. The believe that a healthy nature will heal itself goes very nicely together with the aim to protect nature against destruction and to fight global warming. Those attitudes have more supporters in southern Germany then in northern Germany, and that includes areas like ours: Bavaria!

For Ute and me it was difficult to see each other during those two years of the pandemic, but of course, there always is the telephone and the internet. As always, our conversations cover every aspect of our lives from the very trivial to the great questions of our time. And as always, our live-long feeling of closeness and understanding is unbroken.

Acknowledgement

Normally I write in German, but on this occasion our friend Eileen Cox made me write this down in English, which was quite a challenge. I am thankful to her not only for the idea for this book but for all the help I received from her to find the right expressions (not to talk about the grammar!).
Equally I have to thank many British friends for going through the manuscript, pointing out mistakes or misunderstandings and through their questions making me aware what should perhaps be explained in more detail.
 So especially to all our neighbours and friends on Loch Torridon: thank you for your neighbourly friendliness over so many years and all the good advice I received for this book!